To your success

www.CEO-OnDemand.com.au
www.MoreProfitLessTime.com

THE ENTREPRENEUR'S GUIDE SERIES

HOW TO MASTER THE "BIG 3" IN BUSINESS

Sales & Marketing, Management, and Business Planning

JOHN MILLAR

Thank you to my wife, children, family and friends. Your support and encouragement light my path.

© 2015, John Millar

No part of this publication may be reproduced or transmitted in any form or by any means, mechanical or electronic, including photocopying and recording, or by any information storage and retrieval system, without permission in writing from the publisher. Requests for permission or further information should be addressed to the publishers. Book layout and design by JuggernautPress.com

ISBN-13: 978-1514115381
ISBN-10: 1514115387

When facing a difficult management challenge, wouldn't it be great if you could turn to an expert who can give you simple practical advice to help guide you through to the right decision?

Well now you can. John's book is drawn from years of experience based upon his significant business experience, and he has produced an insightful guide on how to "Master The Big 3 in Business" – business planning, marketing & sales and management. Each chapter gives an insightful guide of easy to read and understand approaches and ideas that will help you resolve your critical business problems.

Engagingly written, this solution-focused book addresses the key issues to help your business find its entrepreneurial spirit. The book is designed to help you as managers and leaders hone your problem solving skills in order to make sound judgement calls on critical business issues.

I challenge you to adapt these strategies in this book. They will lead to new thinking, clearer decisions and effective planning. More than anything, they will lead an organisation to successfully compete in any business conditions.

Tony Gleeson
CEO - Membership
Australian Institute of Management

Contents

Introduction — 15
Starting Your Business — 22
   Optimism Abounds — 23

Business Planning — 29
Executive Summary — 29
   What is an Executive Summary? — 29
   Writing an Executive Summary — 30

Business Profile — 31
   Why are you going into Business? — 32
   Mission Statement — 34
   Business Description — 35
   Business Structure — 36
   Business Registration — 39
   Licences & Permits — 40
   Insurance — 41

Market Analysis — 41
   Market Research — 42
   Measuring Market Demand — 45
   Competitor Analysis — 46
   Segmentation, Targeting & Positioning — 47
   Differentiation — 50
   Forecasting Future Demand — 51

Product or Service Description — 52
   Defining Products & Services — 52
   Unique Selling Proposition — 53
   Selecting Suppliers — 54

Strategy & Implementation — 57
   The Four P's of Marketing — 57
   Covering Your Costs — 58
   Types of Pricing — 59
   Distribution — 61
   Competitive Strategies — 63
   Advertising and Promotions — 64

Operating Plan	67
People	*67*
Systems & Processes	*69*
Equipment	*73*
Facilities	*73*
Managing Risks	*75*
Management Team	77
Key Personnel	*77*
Motivating Employees	*79*
Financial Planning	80
Assets	*80*
Liabilities & Equity	*82*
Assessing your Requirements	*82*
Types of Financing	*83*
Government Funding & Assistance	*85*
Obtaining Finance	*85*
Profit & Loss Statement	*87*
Balance Sheet	*88*
Cash Flow Statement	*90*
Budgeting	*90*
Action Plan	91
What is an Action Plan?	*92*
Developing an Action Plan	*92*

Marketing and Sales — 95

What is Marketing?	95
Marketing Philosophy	*95*
Competitive Strategies	*96*
Marketing Objectives	*98*
Unique Selling Proposition (USP)	*101*
Business vs Consumer Markets	*102*
Understanding your Market	104
Identifying Customers	*104*
Identifying Competitors	*106*
PEST Analysis	*108*
Marketing Research	*110*
Understanding Market Trends	*113*

    SWOT Analysis   *114*
    Market Differentiation   *116*
  Marketing Planning   117
    Business Description   *117*
    Market Segmentation   *118*
    Targeting   *119*
    Positioning   *121*
    Marketing Mix   *122*
  Advertising & Promotions   126
    Advertising   *126*
    Direct Mail   *128*
    Personal Selling   *129*
    Sales Promotions   *130*
    Public Relations   *132*
    Internet Marketing   *133*
    Online & Offline Integration   *135*
  Review & Improve   136
    What is an Action Plan?   *137*
    Developing an Action Plan   *137*
    Reviewing KPIs   *138*
    Monitoring Performance   *140*
    Adjusting a Marketing Campaign   *142*

Management   **145**

  Understanding Leadership   145
    What is Leadership?   *145*
    Are Leaders Born or Made?   *147*
    Leadership Theories   *148*
  Leadership & Business   152
    Importance of Leadership   *152*
    Leadership vs Management   *153*
    Leadership Qualities   *155*
    Effective Delegation   *157*
  Motivating Employees   159
    Theories of Motivation   *159*
    Motivating through Job Design   *162*

How to Set Goals	*164*
Power & Politics	166
Influencing Others	*167*
Social Power	*169*
Organisational Politics	*170*
Decision-making & Managing Conflict	172
Models of Decision-making	*172*
Decision-making Styles	*175*
Group Decision-making	*176*
Types of Conflict	*178*
Compromising	*180*
Managing Conflict	*181*

About the Author — 187

Disclaimer — 191
External Sites — *191*
Waiver and Release — *192*

INTRODUCTION

Having been involved in business since 1987 and since then served a multitude of businesses across a plethora of industries around the globe I have found a simple and immutable truth on which there is always one constant – Most people who go into business are great at what they do but what sets the successful from the unsuccessful is their ability to improve HOW they do business.

Over the years I have had the good fortune to talk to business owners in Australia, New Zealand, Thailand, Malaysia, Hong Kong, China, Korea, Japan, the USA and more and regardless of their origin most avoid the subjects of business planning, sales and marketing, and, management with a passion or at best give it a token nod as they speed past on their rush to their next customer.

The reality is that unless you can master these three areas in your business you cannot possibly achieve your potential in business as they are the foundations on which all sustainable and successful businesses are built.

I spend my life helping business owners and their teams achieve their potential and sincerely hope that you take on this, my latest book in The Entrepreneurs Series seriously and steadfastly persevere with the step by step processes you need to follow if you are to be truly effective and achieve the greatness you should in your business.

To illustrate my point, here are 3 testimonials I recently received from a client, a team member and a supplier. Would your team and your suppliers say this about you? If they can't, then this book is precisely what you need.

Testimonial 1

Engaging in the services of John Millar to be my business coach over 4 years ago now has turned out to be one of the smartest businesses decisions I have made to date. At the time we had been in business for almost 3 years and to be honest our business was struggling like many other small businesses do.

Sales and profits were weak and some years we were going backwards. Within the first year of working with John and implementing his proven methods and systems, our sales increased by 25% and more amazingly our gross profit increased by 140%. The following year sales increased a further 30% and profits 40% and each subsequent year we are experiencing growth on growth.

John really delivers on his name "More Profit Less Time". What I have found even more valuable than just growth on our bottom line is the growth I have personally gained in becoming a better business woman. He has taught my team via group training and myself so many invaluable lessons in business. Without this teaching and support from John over the years we would not be where we are today, and may not even be in business at all.

Along this journey with John, I have been privileged to watch John's business expand and grow. This I believe is due to John's attitude of consent and never-ending improvement. John has helped many

INTRODUCTION

small business owners improve their businesses and sanity through his always-improving coaching systems. I have seen John work tirelessly to create his Business Essential Series that makes his proven method available to the masses. In addition, he has developed his follow-on series so that his clients always have something new to learn and improve on. John is also an esteemed public speaker and devotes his time to the growth of numerous charities and community initiatives. Not to mention publishing an Amazon Best Seller book, with a new hit on the way!

Both John and his team have always shown a high level of professionalism with not only myself and business but all people they come in contact with, even when dealing with difficult people or time wasters. I believe this shows that John is a true professional. John's professionalism shows in all of his work material and marketing. Whilst John is very professional, he is still engaging and friendly. Anyone who has worked with John would agree that it is hard not to genuinely like John. John has the ability to be both a teacher and a support network for his clients. I would say that John's likability is just as important as his high level of professionalism. After all, business is all about people and relationships.

John and his team have ethics as a core value to his business, which is clearly defined and unwavering. John not only holds himself accountable to a high level of ethics but also holds his clients accountable to the same level in their own business dealings. John's high standard of ethics has allowed me to feel comfortable in sharing what would be otherwise confidential financial data and business issues and concerns freely with him. Knowing that I could share these details without judgment and knowing that it would remain confidential is one of the many reasons I value working with John. He also has a no-nonsense approach of complete transparency and honesty so you know you are getting the right advice, not just what you want to hear.

John has a long list of core values which I admire and have also duplicated within my own business and life. John always acts from a place that is in line with his core values that never imposes on another person's values. I admire that his business values are not separate from his life values; he has made his values always serve both. Even without reading his values and Mission Statement it is clear from the moment you meet John that he is passionate and deeply values helping people, improving businesses, and his family and charity and community work!

Thanks...

Testimonial 2

I have been working for John Millar for over a year now and love how he treats his employees as family. He pushes me how to be better at my job, how to expand my network and encourages me to think outside the box.

In a nutshell, I have learned a lot of things from him. His thoughts, advice and love of good business flow through me.

He is not the type of business consultant who needs to seek assistance from a pool of telemarketers just to put up a sale. The good experiences that our existing clients have with him as their coach and business trainer/mentor roll into regular, on going referrals and have expanded his network - and this continues to grow.

If a business mentor/coach does not live by his own words, then he's not a true mentor, or an effective coach at all. John adheres to very strict levels of professionalism and extremely high standards – something he sets for himself to stand out in his industry.

INTRODUCTION

I love how easy he is to listen to and how passionate he is about his work. He creates real relationships with the people he comes into contact with. I am happy I am working under his umbrella.

I've had the opportunity to work with several clients, but it is only with him that I have experienced the way it is to really work with a business mentor. His values are outstanding. His business knowledge, passion and innovation are inspiring.

Christine Rianne
Executive Assistant to John Millar - Certified Business Advisor, Business Consultant, Professional Speaker & Elite Business Trainer International Best Selling Author and Managing Director of:

    www.ceo-ondemand.com.au
    www. moreprofitlesstime.com
    www.moreprofitlesstime.net

More Profit Less Time | Bobarni International Pty Ltd | CEO-ONDEMAND Suite 3/333 Wantirna Road, VIC 3152 Australia | PO Box 6040 Vermont South VIC 3133 Australia E: christine@moreprofitlesstime.com | P: 03 9018 5699

Testimonial 3

I have worked as a copywriter for 18 years and have worked closely with John Millar at More Profit, Less Time for about 18 months.

I have been able to see the continuing growth of his business first-hand, as my own copywriting work has helped him re-vamp his already successful business website, as well as create professional templates for a number of uses within his business.

I have also been working with John as an editor on his soon-to-be-published book – something I feel sure will be another great success, as his previously published books have been.

John is serous about his business and works tirelessly to find new ways to innovate and grow – ensuring he is producing quality written communications that enable him to push his business to the next level of successful growth.

Growth for John is about more than just himself, as the core of his business is focused on the professional growth of others – something John works very positively towards for all his coaching clients at More Profit, Less Time.

Having run my own business for a number of years, I have dealt with a great number of business owners and corporate CEOs.

John's professionalism and attention to detail would rival them all – it is rare to meet someone so focused on their business and someone who works so earnestly to create a business that runs professionally and smoothly.

While many other business owners I deal with through my copywriting work do not value professionally written copy, John accepts nothing less than 100% error-free content in all his marketing materials – the sign of someone committed to professionalism in the way his business image is presented.

My own dealings with him have always shown John to be purely professional – he briefs me clearly, is always polite and respectful and, when it comes to the way he markets his business, he knows what he wants and needs and always pays his invoices on time too.

John has a definite vision for his own professional brand personality

INTRODUCTION

and he is always looking to the leaders in the local and international market to ensure he keeps ahead of his competitors to gain the best possible results for all the clients he takes on. I see this in the written copy I help him create for his business and I see this in the way he communicates with me – a professional who really knows his industry.

John's business ethics are something he showcases proudly in his written communications with clients – something I see first-hand, as the person who works with him to create these documents.

He works in an industry that is unregulated but adheres to an ethical code of conduct he imposes on himself – a very high standard he is committed to meeting and exceeding in every dealing I have had with him.

As I have been responsible for proofreading and editing so much of the course material that John produces for his coaching clients, I am very familiar with his own business values and the ways in which he conveys these to clients.

Part of John's role as a business coach is to help other business owners understand their own values and he is committed to educating all his clients about the importance of good values and how the adherence to these values is the cornerstone of any successful business.

John's role as a business coach and educator puts him in the position of being privy to a lot of sensitive information about the dealings of other business owners – everything from income to debt, to cash flow and employee relations.

John is completely discreet with this information and also very honest.

Rather than giving people false hope about their business which could see them continue as his paying client, John is politely direct and delivers practical, genuine tips on what they should do in their business – even if that means they walk away from it…and him.

This is a great display of his personal and professional values and he really does seem to put people first.

Claire Halliday – Chief Writer, Copy Queens

www.copyqueens.com.au

Starting Your Business

Since I first went into business over 26 years ago, I have seen far too many great people with great ideas go belly up and fail where other less competent and less talented individuals have survived. Some of this is simply due to pure dumb luck, and believe me I have seen some dummies get very lucky, but in the vast majority of cases, the reason a person succeeds or fails lies at the feet of the Rule of 6 P's:

"**P**rior **P**reparation **P**revents **P**itifully **P**oor **P**erformance!"

You could also say it this way: "An ounce of preparation will save you pounds of pain later."

This is top quality advice when applied to starting your own business, where you have so much to gain—and so much to lose. Think of starting a business as being comparable to building a home for your family. If you do not build the foundations correctly, the main structure will collapse and you could lose everything, not just your property, but other less evident things as well. I have seen people who suffered not only a business failure, but also the loss of their family, their fortune, their self-esteem, their dignity—and yes, in some instances, even their lives.

Here is an example of this that I will never forget. Several years back, I was referred to a business owner who was in some amount of trouble making ends meet. After spending just a short amount of time discussing my services, this potential client decided there was no need for a business coach at all, so we parted ways. A few months later, I happened to see a news report about this individual, who had been killed in a terrible car accident. The business was at that point insolvent. On the home front, things were also bad: the spouse had left the home, apparently distraught (according to the news report) after years of angst over the lack of money and the many hours they had spent on the failing business. This business owner ultimately turned to drugs and alcohol and wasn't accepting support from peers, many of whom had disavowed this person.

I know this story is sad, and I can't say for certain that the failed business led to such a terrible ending, but having first-hand knowledge of this person, and listening to the details of the news report did, in my mind, make it a high probability that the failed business venture was in large part to blame.

Optimism Abounds

It is often difficult for a new business owner to see all the potential pitfalls associated with a startup because they have so much enthusiasm for the venture and an unquenchable desire to be their own boss. In the eyes of the founder, business ownership has many benefits because success in business can lead to extreme wealth and (what appears to be) complete control over one's destiny. In reality, however, even the most successful business founders are never in complete control of their destiny because they still answer to someone or something. It may not be an overbearing boss standing at the doorway to an office full of cubicles demanding that you arrive every morning at 8 a.m. sharp; instead, it could a $10-million-dollar-a-year client needed by the business owner for the company to remain successful. As with most things in life, the "equation" of business ownership has both an upside and a downside as well.

Now that I have given you some of the doom and gloom,

we can move on with the task at hand: showing you how to start a company properly. I will share with you some of what I share with a typical client who comes to me for coaching or consulting when they are planning to start a new business.

First of all, you must understand that it really doesn't matter how many companies a person has owned in the past (I have owned so many I have lost count). You must still follow the basic rules of business, and most of all it comes down to *planning*. As the old saying goes (and I'm sure you have heard it many times):

"If you fail to plan you plan to fail"

What should a person do to gain the knowledge needed to start a business?

Basically, you can take classes, read books, or get direction from a competent business coach or mentor. The biggest problem with getting this information from books is that so many books say a lot about nothing and nothing about a lot, or they are so busy force-feeding their information that a reader doesn't know where to start. Add to that a countless number of coaches, who are essentially unskilled "vermin" and "predators" who spend all day promising the entire planet while delivering very little. These are the so-called "business coaches" and "consultants" that have no real business sense or valid experience. In many instances, the only business they ever owned is their coaching or consulting business. Add to this the plethora of misinformation out there about what is actually required to start and run a successful business, and you start to see why (1) more businesses fail in the first two years of operation than survive, and (2) of those that do survive, the vast majority won't be around after five years.

I have written this book in simple English, making sure to present the basic steps in the order you must follow to start

INTRODUCTION

your business properly. The book offers a lot of information, but it also challenges you with many relevant questions. Take the time to think about and answer these questions carefully, and they will provide you with many of the answers you need to not only *survive* but to *thrive* in today's highly competitive marketplace.

I know your task is difficult. I coach business owners every day who are facing the same problems you will likely face when starting your business. The good news is that most of these problems can be overcome—or avoided entirely—if you start your business with a good foundation and proper planning. You can do so by soliciting advice EARLY ON from a competent business coach, accountant, and lawyer; then, as your business evolves, your team of helpers can evolve along with it.

Whether you are planning to start your 1st business or your 50th business, let me be your guide. Walk with me on this exciting new journey. Grab a pen, notepad, and highlighters; then get ready to knuckle down and do it right the first time while we turn your idea into a multi-million dollar, highly profitable business together.

John L Millar
AIMM - Dip Mgmt - Dip Hrm - Cert IV TAE - NLP Prac
Certified Business Advisor, Business Consultant, Professional Speaker & Elite Business Trainer
International Best Selling Author and Managing Director of:

    www.ceo-ondemand.com.au
    www. moreprofitlesstime.com

Finalist - 2014 Australian Institute of Management Business Excellence Awards
Nominee - 2015 Australian Institute of Management Business Excellence Awards
Nominee - 2015 Telstra Business Awards

Nominee - 2015 Small Business Awards
Nominee - 2015 IPPY Award
Finalist - 2015 Axiom Business Book Award
Nominee - 2015 Australian Small Business Champion Award

NOTES

www.CEO-OnDemand.com.au
www.MoreProfitLessTime.com

NOTES

www.CEO-OnDemand.com.au
www.MoreProfitLessTime.com

BUSINESS PLANNING

Executive Summary

Do you know what an executive summary of a business plan is and why it is so important to your future business success? What better way to start a business-building book than with this key information...

In this chapter, you'll discover the answer to these questions, PLUS benefit from practical guidance to help you create an effective executive summary for your own business.

What is an Executive Summary?

An executive summary is the first part of your Business Plan that people will read. First impressions matter, don't they? For this reason, it is very important the impact you make encourages people to continue and read the rest of your plan. The alternative? That they make a decision to not bother looking any further – and that's no good for your business.

The executive summary gives an outline of what is contained in the full plan document, with enough information for readers to understand the key points, what is unique about your business and why your business will be successful.

The executive summary will usually also contain a concise but powerful description of your business, an overview of your products and/or services, a general outline of your target market, industry and competitors, as well as an overview of key factors that will make your business a success.

Writing an Executive Summary

The executive summary is generally written last - after you have completed development and writing of the full plan document. This ensures you allow the plan to evolve, with full analysis of all issues and without pre-empting any areas with a premature summary that locks you into something that has not been fully evaluated.

While you don't write the full executive summary until the end, it can be helpful to first write a brief outline or draft of an executive summary before you develop the full plan.

This gives you a guideline to follow when creating your business plan to ensure that you don't leave out any information.

After completing the rest of your business plan, go back to your original draft and finalise what you plan to include in your executive summary.

Keep in mind that the objective is to make the reader believe that you have a business proposition that will be successful.

When you're ready to write your executive summary, stay focused – making sure you highlight the main points that you would like to get across to the reader.

These points should showcase your unique selling proposition (USP), or what it is that will make your business a success in the marketplace.

Remember to avoid going into too much detail in the executive summary - the rest of the business plan is for the details. Depending on the length of your business plan, aim to keep your executive summary to less than one page.

Now it's time to edit, proofread and revise.

Continue to review and modify your executive summary until you feel that it meets its objectives. It is also important to get other people to review your business plan - especially your executive summary – paying special attention on clarity and professionalism, including basic grammar, spelling and punctuation errors. When in doubt, engage the services of a trusted copywriter or professional proofreader.

Build your Business Planning plan

Build your business plan by answering the questions at the end of each section. A plan will automatically be generated, based on your responses.

Executive Summary

Q.1 Write a summary based on the contents of your business plan. It should briefly outline each section of your business plan and contain some form of mission statement.

This should only be completed once you have finished your business plan.

Business Profile

Next? Now it's time to develop the part of your business plan that builds a profile on your business.

The knowledge shared in this chapter provides you with an opportunity to reflect on your motivation, by considering your reasons for going into business in the first place.

An effective business profile will enable you to articulate what type of business you have and what aims you will strive to achieve. It also describes the legal requirements for setting up your business, including business structure, registration, licenses and permit obligations, as well as insurance.

You can use this handy, truly practical information to help you as you work through the development of your business plan.

Why are you going into Business?

Running your own business can be very rewarding BUT there will be many more challenges to encounter along the way. Identifying your particular reasons for going into business will help you to develop a clear vision for what you want your business to achieve in the future – and, importantly, what you, personally, want to get out of it.

What reasons do you have for starting your business? You can use the reasons listed below as a starting point to help you assess your situation, or develop your own reasons that are uniquely relevant to your individual circumstances.

Typical reasons for going into business;
- » To make an income
- » To gain control over your career
- » You have an idea for a business
- » You want to have control over your own work environment
- » To have more flexible working hours
- » You enjoy working for yourself and leading other people
- » To generate an income and jobs for your community

Before deciding whether or not you should run your own business, you should also be aware of the many challenges and risks you may face as a new business owner. A thorough understanding of these issues will assist you in your decision.

What are some of the challenges business owners may face?

We've listed some below:
Initial funding –

Starting a new business often requires some form of capital outlay. You should consider things such as facilities, equipment, hiring staff, and any marketing efforts. If you don't have the necessary funding, you may have to seek assistance from other sources of finance, such as banks, investors, and even family and friends.

Cash flow –

A profitable business does not necessarily translate to a positive cash flow. For example, customers may purchase your product or service on credit, or you will have to spend money to purchase supplies and equipment for a job up front. To ensure a positive cash flow, you should implement a credit management system and offer incentives for faster payments.

Market saturation –

Undertaking market research is a critical success factor for all businesses. A highly saturated market would mean increased competition for your business. Even if you think you have a unique product or service, you won't be sure until you conduct some market research. This can be undertaken by yourself, or you may choose to seek the services of a professional.

Product awareness –

If consumers are unaware of your product or service, they won't be able to purchase from you. In order to successfully reach your target market, you have to implement a marketing strategy, consisting of market segmentation, targeting and advertising and promotional activities.

Staffing –

As your employees will be dealing with customers and representing your business, it is important to ensure they can perform the job at a high calibre. To get the right staff, you should follow a carefully considered recruitment process plan, or seek the services of a HR recruitment agency. Some things you may want to consider include: skills, experiences, qualifications, expectations and responsibilities.

Suppliers –

If your business is dependent on having on-time delivery of supplies, such as retail shops or restaurants, it is essential to carefully select your suppliers to ensure their reliability. Failure to do so may lead to an under-stock of supplies and, consequently, decrease your profits.

Time management –

If you've worked a 9-5 job your whole life and then decide to start your own business, you may become overwhelmed with the amount of work and responsibilities involved. For example, you might be responsible for opening and closing, ensuring tidiness of shop/office, paying the bills, checking accounts, and monitoring stock levels. Therefore, it is essential that you have good time management and learn how to prioritise your activities.

Mission Statement

It is important to have a goal for what you want your business to achieve. A mission statement can be used to determine this, as it sets out the broad objectives of your business.

Developing a sound mission for your business will communicate its purpose to consumers, employees and the market (including finance providers, investors and competitors).

A mission statement is generally only five or six lines long and sets out the main , most unique qualities of your business.

A mission statement defines the following:
- » What does your business sell? - Incorporating what is special or unique about your product or service.

- » Who are the business stakeholders? - That is, who is impacted by the operational success of the business (customers, investors, employees, etc).
- » What distinguishes your business from others in the marketplace? - This involves defining your competitive advantage in the market.
- » What benefits are provided to customers? - This includes meeting consumer needs and providing solutions to demands.
- » What are the broad principles that your business will practice to ensure customer satisfaction? – Detail your business standards and ethics, including quality, competitiveness, flexibility, etc.

Build your Business Planning plan

Build your business plan by answering the questions below. A plan will automatically be generated, based on your responses.

Business Objectives

Q.1 What are your objectives, in terms of revenue?

Q.2 What are your objectives, in terms of your market share?

Q.3 What are your objectives, in terms of your product/service?

Business Description

A business description allows you to get your ideas, plans and visions down on paper before you go any further. It is important to have a thorough understanding of what your business is, and the direction that you intend it to follow.

To help you develop your business description, you can brainstorm all of your ideas about what your business will be and the products and services you will provide to consumers.

Some questions to consider when brainstorming include:
- » What is the main purpose of your business?
- » What products and services will your business provide?
- » Who will be your customers/suppliers?
- » What will your role be within the business?
- » Does your business have future growth potential?
- » How profitable could the business become?
- » What will the business be in five years time?

The business description does not need to be overly extensive or detailed. It is mainly to provide an outline of what will be explored further in the business plan.

Build your Business Planning plan

Build your business plan by answering the questions below. A plan will automatically be generated, based on your responses.

Business Profile

Q.1 What is your business' trading name?

Q.2 Are you starting a new business, buying an established business, starting a franchise, or are you an independent contractor?

Q.3 Describe the ownership of the business.

Q.4 Describe the products/services that your business will offer.

Q.5 Where will your business be located?

Q.6 Why is this location ideal?

Business Structure

When deciding on a structure, it is important to consider

the nature of your business, including factors such as:

» Type of business
» Tax liability
» Ease of set-up and set-up costs
» Asset protection

The following is a brief description of the various types of business structures available:

Sole trader

A sole trader is a business owned and managed by one individual who is solely responsible for the business' debts and legal obligations. Sole traders have minimal reporting obligations and relatively low establishment costs.

Partnership

A partnership is where between 2 and 20 people co-own a business and carry out the business activities together, with a view to profit. The co-owners share in the business' assets, liabilities and profits, in accordance with a partnership agreement, with the partnership agreement establishing partner responsibilities, entitlements to profits and share of business ownership.

Company

A company is a separate legal entity, that is, its owners are regarded as separate from the business. For this reason, the business can change ownership and continue to run, despite the original owners leaving the business. Further, the company owners have limited liability for the business' debts.

Co-operative

A co-operative is a jointly-owned commercial enterprise with at least five members who own and control the organisation. It produces and distributes goods and services and is run with the aim of meeting the needs of its members for the benefit of its owners. A good example of a co-operative is a farmer cooperative where there are a number of dairy farmers, for example, who join forces and sell their product under the same brand.

Incorporated association

An incorporated association is an inexpensive and simpler structure for a small, not-for-profit community-based organisation. Such an association is set up under the Associations Incorporation Act 1984. Incorporation, similarly to a company, ensures the association is a separate legal entity from its members and, hence, members cannot be sued individually for their personal assets, as their liability is limited to the capital they invested into the association.

Trust

The concept of a trust revolves around the idea of property being held by one party (the trustee) on behalf of another (the beneficiary). A trust can have tax advantages, depending on how the trust is structured, and may have a greater level of asset protection than other business structures.

Franchising

Franchising is when you pay fees and royalties to the parent company of the franchise in return for the right to sell the franchise's products and sell under the franchiser's well-known trade name.

Build your Business Planning plan

Build your business plan by answering the questions below. A plan will automatically be generated, based on your responses.

Business Profile

Q.1 What is the legal structure of your business?

Q.2 Why have you chosen this structure?

Business Registration

Depending on the business structure you select, there are different business registration requirements.

Registering a business name

For any structure other than a company, a business name must always be registered with the appropriate state or territory government office. You can use your own name as your business name, for example "John Smith", however, you can't build on your name, such as "John Smith's Gardening Service".

If you are planning to trade only within one state or territory, or sell over the internet, then you only need to register your business within that state or territory. However, if you are going to trade in another state or territory, then you will need to register your business name with them also.

If you decide on a company business structure, you only need to register your company before you can conducting business in any state and territory. In doing this, you have the advantage of having your company name registered nation-wide. However, if you choose to operate using another business name, then you will need to register that name with the appropriate state or territory.

When choosing a business name, it should be distinctive from other businesses and simple to remember. You need to make sure that the name you select is not already registered, or too similar to another name that is already registered.

Registering your domain name

If you decide to set up a business website and email, your domain is what identifies your business on the internet and is an important marketing tool. To purchase a .com.au or a .net.au domain name in Australia, you must first possess an Australian Company Number or Australian Business Number, so it pays to check what you require where you live.

Register your trademark

Registering a trademark gives you the exclusive right to use it Australia-wide as part of your brand image and legally prevents others from using it. Trademark registration can last for an initial 10-year period and needs to be re-registered thereafter. If you are considering registering your trademark internationally, you must register it in each country you want it protected in.

Licences & Permits

Prior to starting your business, it is important to make yourself aware of any applicable licenses and permits. This will ensure that you are able to commence trading when the appropriate time comes. There are regulations from all levels of government; federal, state and local.

Licences and permits that your business may be required to possess in Australia include:

- » Australian Business Number (ABN)
- » Workers' Compensation
- » Superannuation Guarantee
- » GST Registration
- » Tax File Number

You will need to find all the licenses and permits required at federal and state level for your business and other details that are relevant to where you are setting up. You may also need to contact your local council to check for any business restrictions or licenses and permits required – especially if you are running a business from home.

Build your Business Planning plan

Build your business plan by answering the questions below. A plan will automatically be generated, based on your responses.

Business Profile

Q.1 Identify and describe any licenses/permits required to run your business.

Q.2 Are there any other regulatory issues that need to be addressed?

Insurance

Risk is the probability of being exposed to an unfavorable event, which could result in financial or other loss. All businesses are exposed to risk, however insurance can be secured to help manage it.

There are three different types of insurance;

- » **Asset and Revenue Insurance** - this insurance is for the protection of your assets and your ability to generate revenue
- » **People Insurance** - this insurance protects you and your employees from loss due to accident, injury or illness
- » **Liability Insurance** - this insurance protects you against different forms of liability, such as public liability, professional liability and product liability.

It is important to note that some insurance products, such as workers' compensation are mandatory for all businesses in Australia. You can research and seek professional advice to determine the different types of insurance and the appropriate level of insurance cover you need for your business.

It is also worthwhile investigating each insurance provider, to compare policies.

Market Analysis

In this chapter, you'll explore how to develop the part of the business plan that builds a profile of your business. It focuses on understanding the market and where your business fits best, along with practical insights into developing competitive strategies.

You can use this information to help you as you work through the development of your business plan.

Market Research

Market research involves collecting, organising, analysing and communicating information that can be used in order to make an informed marketing decision. Performing market research will complement your marketing mix strategy, as it enables you to make educated decisions regarding selecting markets, your image or branding and products or services.

There are five key steps to conducting market research:

Define the Problem

In this stage, you need to identify the actual problems that are relating to the apparent symptoms. For example, poor sales within a business are not the problem - they are the symptom of a larger issue, such as a weak marketing strategy.

Further business problems may include:

- » Who are your target customers?
- » What method could be implemented to reach these customers?
- » Who are your customers and what advantages and disadvantages do they have over your business?
- » What size is the consumer market you are trying to engage?

Collect the Data

There are two types of market research that can be performed:

- » ***Primary research*** - involves collecting information from sources directly by conducting interviews and surveys, and by talking to customers and established businesses.

» ***Secondary research*** - involves collecting information from sources where the primary research has already been conducted. Such information includes industry statistics, market research reports, newspaper articles, etc.

There are also a number of different collection methods and techniques, such as qualitative and quantitative research.

Qualitative research is where you seek an understanding of why things are a certain way. For example, a researcher may stop a shopper and ask them why they bought a particular product or brand.

Quantitative research refers to measuring market phenomena in a numerical sense, such as when a bank asks consumers to rate their service on a scale of one to ten.

Analyse and interpret the data

You must attach meaning to the data you have collected during your market research to make sense of it and to develop alternative solutions that could potentially solve your business problem. You should determine how the knowledge you have gained through researching your market can be applied and used to develop effective business strategies.

Reach a conclusion

With the alternatives you have developed to solve your problem in mind, perform a cost-benefit analysis of each alternative, keeping in mind the potentially limited resources available to your business. You may also need to perform further investigation into each alternative solution to arrive at the best decision for your business in regards to meeting consumer demands.

Implement your research

Put your final solution into practice. Without completing this step, your research could potentially have been a waste of your time and resources. Further, ensure you communicate your plan to your employees to ensure they are informed, can put your solution into practice, and monitor results.

Build your Business Planning plan

Build your business plan by answering the questions below. A plan will automatically be generated, based on your responses.

Business Profile

Q.1 List some of the opportunities that exist for your business.

Q.2 List some of the threats that exist for your business.

Q.3 List some of the weaknesses of your business.

Q.4 List some of the strengths of your business.

Market Analysis

Q.5 Is this industry governed by legislation?

Q.6 What trends may affect this industry in the future and how?

Q.7 What current trends are affecting the industry?

Q.8 What trends have previously affected this industry?

Q.9 What are some of the technological factors that may affect your business?

Q.10 What are some of the social and cultural factors that may affect your business?

Q.11 What are some of the economic factors that may affect your business?

Q.12 What are some of the political and legal factors that may affect your business?

Q.13 What types of market research have you undertaken?

Q.14 How far back will your research go?

Q.15 What impact does it have on the industry and the success of your business?

Measuring Market Demand

Defining the demand for your product within the wider consumer market is an important step in market analysis.

You'll have the solid foundations you need to develop effective strategies to promote and sell your product to as many potential customers as possible.

Market demand is the total volume of a product or service that would be bought by a consumer group, where the location, time period and marketing effort are defined. Market demand can depend on environmental factors as well, such as the sales of a related product or service or the current economic conditions.

Base line market demand is called the market minimum. This refers to the number of sales that would occur, regardless of any marketing efforts or underlying factors. There is also a limit to market demand that is referred to as 'market potential'. Market potential is where an increased marketing effort, even combined with other factors, would have no effect on overall sales.

Market demand can also be divided into two categories:

» Primary
» Selective demand

Primary demand is the total demand for all brands of a given product or service. Selective demand is the demand for a given brand of product or services.

A business should estimate what its share of the market

could be, in order to assess its business potential.

Once you have analysed the entire potential market for your product, study your competitors and their customers. Then gauge what amount of this market you can realistically see your business capturing.

To measure market demand, you can use published industry statistics, surveys or even by spying on your competitors and compiling a list of how many customers they have and how many sales they make.

Using this knowledge, you can estimate what the market demand for your business will be.

The market demand of your business is equal to your potential market share multiplied by the total market demand.

Competitor Analysis

To be able to effectively gain an understanding of the market you are preparing to enter, it is vital to have an in-depth knowledge of your competitors. The better that you understand the competition, the more effective the strategies you can make to compete with them.

Essentially, if your product is something that people want, you will have little trouble selling it, provided that there are no competitors. However, there are almost always competitors, or at least there soon will be if a product is successful. These competitors will either make a similar product in a way that makes it superior to yours, or they will undercut you on price and offer better value to the customer.

Understanding your competitors will also help you to develop a better understanding of your customers. You can learn the reasons that customers buy from competitors as well as understanding what strategies the competition use to market to these people.

Competitor Analysis can be performed using two methods. You can observe your competitors first-hand as a customer yourself, entering their stores and utilising their services to see how they operate.

You may also choose to talk to the customers of a competing business and find out directly from them what makes them choose one business over another. It could be value, quality, service, reputation, indifference or simply habit.

Build your Business Planning plan

Build your business plan by answering the questions below. A plan will automatically be generated based on your responses.

Market Analysis

Q.1 Identify three of your major competitors.

Q.2 Identify the products/services that they offer.

Q.3 Describe the products/services that they offer.

Q.4 What factors contribute to their success?

Q.5 Assess their weaknesses.

Q.6 How will you address their strengths and capitalise on their weaknesses?

Q.7 What are their current market shares?

Segmentation, Targeting & Positioning

In order to be an effective and efficient business, you should seek out your target customer market. There are three main issues to consider when determining your target market:

Market segmentation

Market segmentation involves grouping your various customers into segments that have common needs or will respond similarly to a marketing action. Each segment will respond to a different marketing mix strategy, with each offering alternate growth and profit opportunities.

Some different ways you can segment your market include

the following;

» Demographics which focus on the characteristics of the customer. For example age, gender, income bracket, education, job and cultural background.
» Psychographics which refer to the customer group's lifestyle. For example, their social class, lifestyle, personality, opinions, and attitudes.
» Behaviour which is based on customer behaviour. For example, online shoppers, shopping centre customers, brand preference and prior purchases.
» Geographical location such as continent, country, state, province, city or rural area that the customer group resides.

Targeting

After segmenting the market based on the different groups and classes, you will need to choose your targets. No one strategy will suit all consumer groups, so being able to develop specific strategies for your target markets is very important.

There are three general strategies for selecting your target markets:

» ***Undifferentiated Targeting:*** This approach views the market as one group with no individual segments, therefore using a single marketing strategy. This strategy may be useful for a business or product with little competition where you may not need to tailor strategies for different preferences.
» ***Concentrated Targeting:*** This approach focuses on selecting a particular market niche on which marketing efforts are targeted. Your firm is focusing on a single segment so you can concentrate on understanding the needs and wants of that particular market intimately. Small firms often benefit from this

strategy as focusing on one segment enables them to compete effectively against larger firms.
» *Multi-Segment Targeting:* This approach is used if you need to focus on two or more well defined market segments and want to develop different strategies for them. Multi segment targeting offers many benefits but can be costly as it involves greater input from management, increased market research and increased promotional strategies.

Prior to selecting a particular targeting strategy, you should perform a cost benefit analysis between all available strategies and determine which will suit your situation best.

Positioning

Positioning is developing a product and brand image in the minds of consumers. It can also include improving a customer's perception about the experience they will have if they choose to purchase your product or service. The business can positively influence the perceptions of its chosen customer base through strategic promotional activities and by carefully defining your business' marketing mix.

Effective positioning involves a good understanding of competing products and the benefits that are sought by your target market.

It also requires you to identify a differential advantage with which it will deliver the required benefits to the market effectively against the competition. Business should aim to define themselves in the eyes of their customers in regards to their competition.

Build your Business Planning plan

Build your business plan by answering the questions below.

Market Analysis

Q.1 Identify and describe the various market segments.

Q.2 Will you be targeting a business market, consumer market, or both?

Q.3 Will the target market be local, national, international, or a mix?

Q.4 Describe the types of people you want to reach.

Q.5 What role do they play in the decision making process?

Q.6 What factors stimulate and influence their buying patterns?

Q.7 Will your product/service meet the needs of the target market? If so, how?

Q.8 Describe your strategy for approaching the target market.

Q.9 What is the positioning strategy for your product/service?

Differentiation

The process of developing business, product and service differentiation is important as it allows you to set yourself apart from the rest of the market. This can be particularly important where an extremely competitive market exists or where there are a limited number of customers to sell to.

In order to differentiate yourself from the competition, you need to conduct market analysis into both what the main players in the market are doing, as well as what you could do differently. You then need to develop a strategy that takes both of these factors into consideration.

Differentiating your business from your competitors is an ongoing process. You may be able to be innovative and provide products and services beyond what your competition can initially, however, the competition will soon catch up.

A business needs to be able to develop and move forward

if it wants to stay ahead of its competitors for a sustained period of time.

Another method of differentiation is to provide a product or service that is different and innovative or simply of better quality or value. It is very difficult to differentiate certain products as there is often little opportunity for variation. There are a range of factors that you can use to differentiate a product or service, including performance, style, design, functionality, quality, value, reliability and durability.

While differentiation can be a useful tool to separate one business from another, it is important to keep in mind that customers generally don't like something different for the sake of it.

There is no point in changing your business if the sole reason you are doing it is to differentiate yourself from the rest of the market.

You need to ensure that what you offer is in some way better than what the competition provides.

Forecasting Future Demand

Forecasting is the process of estimating future demand by anticipating what customers are likely to do given a certain set of conditions. Forecasting can give you an advantage over your competitors during periods of market change.

Unfortunately, very few products, services, industries or markets are easy to forecast. This is because very few markets follow consistent cycles and there are a range of external and environmental factors that can cause changes to market demand.

The more unstable the market, the better your forecasting will need to be.

The way to counter this is to have projections for a range of different circumstances. These projections can be based on indicators such as interest rates, inflation, market trends, changing consumer tastes and unemployment. Therefore, you can plan for and have strategies prepared to either survive tough times or be aggressive and increase your market share.

The benefits of conducting realistic forecasting are that you can reduce surplus inventory whilst ensuring that you have enough stock to meet demand. This means that you can avoid the costs associated with having excess or wasted stock as well as capitalise on making as many sales as possible.

There are a number of methods that you can implement in order to forecast the future market demand.

Customer surveys will allow you to gain an understanding of what your customers believe the future holds for them, your business and the market.

Analysis of the leading market indicators, expert opinion and past sales analysis can also help you to forecast future market demand.

Product or Service Description

This chapter helps you to develop the part of the business that is related to developing the products and services that your business will offer. It will also describe what needs to be taken into consideration when selecting suppliers.

You can use this information to help you as you work through the development of your business plan.

Defining Products & Services

To help you accurately define and develop the products and services that you will take to the market, you can create a product description statement.

When writing a product description statement, ensure that you connect the features of your product to the way that they can benefit customers.

By having a clear understanding of what your product is, you'll be in a better position to fully exploit its potential when advertising and selling it. A clear definition of your product can also help customers make informed decisions and improve their level of satisfaction.

To further improve the attractiveness of your offering you may like to consider adding additional value using incentives such as guarantees and warranties.

A warranty is a legally implied obligation which guarantees the repair or replacement of a product in the event that it fails within a certain period after it has been purchased.

A guarantee is an agreement by the business to assure the quality or length of use of a product offered for sale by the business and in the event that the product is faulty, a refund is given.

Build your Business Planning plan

Build your business plan by answering the questions below. A plan will automatically be generated based on your responses.

Product/Service Overview

Q.1 Describe your products/services.

Unique Selling Proposition

A key point in developing your marketing strategy is to come up with your unique selling proposition (USP).

A USP is what makes your product or service stand out from your competitors and is generally the reason why customers will purchase your product or service over those of the competition.

Some commonly used USPs are offering 'best service', 'lowest price', 'best value' or 'most advanced technology'. However, when determining your product's USP, be sure to also look beyond the physical characteristics of your product and consider the intangible or psychological benefits of the product for your target customer group such as security, comfort, and timeliness.

To convey your USP to customers, you can consider developing it as a way to promote your product. Consider using it on your marketing communications such as business cards, letter heads, brochures, web site etc.

A value-added service is an important factor that should be considered when developing your business' USP.

Value-adding refers to providing a supplementary or complementary benefit to the customer in addition to your core product which the customer wouldn't receive from your competitors. It is an extra incentive used to encourage customers to rate your product above those of your competitors.

Build your Business Planning plan

Build your business plan by answering the questions below. A plan will automatically be generated based on your responses.

Product/Service Overview

Q.1 Identify and describe the points of difference between your product / service and those of your competitors?

Q.2 What is your product's unique selling proposition? i.e. what makes your product different from your competitors?

Selecting Suppliers

Your product or parts of it may be bought in full or made from raw materials that you purchase from suppliers. Working closely and with these suppliers to develop strong relationships and develop efficient business systems to facilitate your purchasing requirements can help you to; increase profitability, maximise efficiencies, optimise your inventory levels, and reduce storage requirements.

When selecting suppliers it is important to carefully evaluate their offering, considering various factors as the following:

Number of Suppliers

Dealing with a single supplier can be very efficient and offer opportunities to forge strategic linkages increasing quantity discounts, levels of cooperation and responsiveness. However, utilising multiple suppliers provides options that protect you against an over-reliance on a single supplier and reduce your risk. Utilising multiple suppliers also provides the opportunity to ensure competitiveness.

Supplier Reliability

Reliability of the supplier is their ability to deliver a quality product to your business on time. Problems with deliveries can cause major disruptions to your business. You can evaluate the reliability of a supplier by asking for their on-time delivery statistics or by using their existing customers as a reference. It is also good practice to start out with a small order when using a new supplier so you can evaluate their performance.

Evaluating prices

It is well worth spending time to research different suppliers to gain an understanding of the range of services and prices on offer. You can then negotiate final pricing and payment terms with the suppliers to ensure you receive the best possible deal.

Additional Services

This involves the supplier's ability to assist your business to coordinate your inventory control systems and ordering processes. Developing close links and even integrated ordering systems can be a good way to improve supply efficiencies and reduce procurement costs. If this is managed effectively, there can be benefits for both your business and your suppliers.

Intellectual Property

Intellectual property (IP) is the product of someone's intellect, used to create something novel, different or original. It can occur in a number of forms, such as a piece of art work, a good idea, a design or plans for a design, an invention, knowledge, a book or a trade secret.

IP can be legally secured to ensure that only a certain person (or group of persons) have exclusive rights and control over the use of the idea or invention and therefore have rights to extract profits from it if they see fit.

It is illegal for others to copy or use that idea or invention for their own benefit.

There are a number of methods that can be implemented to ensure that your intellectual property rights are protected.

Patents

A patent is the exclusive right given to the owner to commercially exploit the process, design or invention for the life of the patent in return for public disclosure of the process design or invention. You need to apply for a patent before it will be protected by law.

Prior to your patent application being accepted it is examined to ensure it meets the necessary legal requirements. Some things are not patentable by law, such as mathematical formulas and ideas or artistic creations.

Trademarks

Used to identify a unique product or service to distinguish it from business competitors. Examples include a logo, letter, name, shape, picture, sound, aspect of packaging, smell, or a phrase. While you do not need to register the trademark to use it, registration does provide your business with the exclusive rights to use, licence or sell the trademark.

It is important to note that you need to pay a fee for renewal of registration to maintain the trademark.

Copyright

This protects original works of art, writing, music, films, visual images, films and computer programs that express the creator's ideas and information from unauthorised copying. Copyright protection is free and does not need to be registered for.

So, every time you put an original idea or information into a material form it is automatically copyrighted.

However, it is advisable that owners of any original work should place a copyright notice on or near their work.

Strategy & Implementation

This chapter describes various product pricing techniques, product distribution methods, PLUS it discusses the various advertising and promotional options available to your business – many at low or no-cost.

The Four P's of Marketing

Marketing is a business function that identifies consumer needs, determines target markets and applies products and services to serve these markets. It also involves promoting such products and services within the marketplace.

Marketing is integral to the success of any business, large or small, with its primary focus on quality, consumer value and customer satisfaction. A strategy commonly utilised is the "Marketing Mix". This tool is made up of four variables known as the "Four P's" of marketing.

The marketing mix blends these variables together to produce the results it wants to achieve in its specific target market.

The following describes the four Ps of marketing:

Product

Products are the goods and services that your business

provides for sale to your target market. When developing a product you should consider quality, design, features, packaging, customer service and any subsequent after-sales service.

Place

Place is in regards to distribution, location and methods of getting the product to the customer. This includes the location of your business, shop front, distributors, logistics and the potential use of the internet to sell products directly to consumers.

Price

Price concerns the amount of money that customers must pay in order to purchase your products. There are a number of considerations in relation to price including price setting, discounting, credit and cash purchases as well as credit collection.

Promotion

Promotion refers to the act of communicating the benefits and value of your product to consumers. It then involves persuading general consumers to become customers of your business using methods such as advertising, direct marketing, personal selling and sales promotion.

Covering Your Costs

When it comes to determining a price for your products, it is important to ensure that you are able to cover all of the costs involved in bringing the product to the market whilst also leaving a margin from which to make a profit.

It is also important to consider what your target market is and what they are prepared to spend.

In general, there are three types of costs you need to consider;

Fixed Costs

The expenditures that do not change regardless of the business's volume of sales. These must be covered no matter what sales you achieve. Examples include rent, licence fees and interest to be paid on business debts.

These depend on the operational activities of the business. That is, as the volume of sales and production activities change, so does the level of costs. Examples include material costs that are inputs to the production process.

These depend on the operational activities of the business. That is, as the volume of sales and production activities change, so does the level of costs. Examples include material costs that are inputs to the production process.

Variable Costs

These depend on the operational activities of the business. That is, as the volume of sales and production activities change, so does the level of costs. Examples include material costs that are inputs to the production process.

Semi Fixed Costs

Are costs that have a fixed component and a variable component such as infrastructure expenses (telephone line rental and usage, electricity, water).

Your pricing should reflect the levels of these costs and cover your expenses at the very least.

In the initial stages of developing a business, profit levels may be low; however you should aim to increase the level of profit as your business grows.

Types of Pricing

It is important to have a pricing strategy that is tailored to your target market.

There are various ways of setting prices as outlined in the following:

Mark-up pricing:

Mark-up is the difference between the costs of producing and selling a product (fixed costs plus variable costs) and the market selling price of the product. It is the difference between what you spend to produce the product and what the customer spends to purchase it.

It is calculated as follows:

» *Fixed Cost per unit* = Total Fixed Cost / Units Produced
» *Variable Cost per unit* = Total Variable Costs / Units Produced
» *Selling Price* = Fixed Cost per unit Variable Cost per unit Desired Profit Margin

Desired profit margin is the amount of profit you would like your business to make above your production costs. It can be expressed as a percentage of the total costs.

Value-based pricing

Value-based pricing sells the product at the price based on the customer's perceived value of the product.

A good example where such a pricing system is used is on luxury items, where the actual value is quite different from the perceived value. For example, a luxury item may not actually cost nearly as much to make as what people are prepared to pay for it.

It is important to note that this method of pricing is based on a sound understanding of how customers judge value and may only be possible after a product has a strong reputation.

Target return pricing

Using this strategy, a business first determines what level of demand there is for the product and then identifies the desired profit the business would like to make from the product. The price is calculated by dividing the total desired profit by the expected level of sales. Therefore, by meeting the level of expected sales, a certain amount of profit will be received.

Going-rate pricing

In the situation where the business is in a competitive market, the business charges the average price of what its competitors are charging for a similar or the same product. This may be the case where there is only a small amount of competition and the product is a necessity.

It is sometimes in a business' best interest to not compete by undercutting their competition.

Build your Business Planning plan

Build your business plan by answering the questions below. A plan will automatically be generated, based on your responses.

Strategy

Q.1 Describe your pricing strategy and how it lines up with your market.

Q.2 Why do you think this strategy will be effective?

Q.3 How competitive is your product/service price, compared with your direct competitors?

Distribution

Distribution refers to the methods that you can implement in order to allow your customers to access or receive their purchases.

There are a number of options to choose from to distribute your products to customers, including:

Direct distribution

Your business sells its products directly to customers through channels such as retail stores, markets, the internet, direct mail orders, door-to-door sales and catalogues.

Indirect distribution

Your business sells its product through some form of middleman, who sells the product on behalf of the business. This may be through retailers (such as department stores), wholesalers, agents (such as a real-estate agent) or a distributor.

The distribution method you choose for your product will be dependent on a number of factors, such as cost and your target market. Each distribution method has positive and negative aspects, so a thorough cost-benefit analysis will go a long way in assisting you to make an informed decision.

Generally, wherever possible, it is good to be able to sell directly to customers. This is because when you introduce a third party to the process, you are taking away some of your control over the customer experience. If your agent does a poor job of distributing your product it can inflict a negative impact on your business. Indirect distribution may also come with additional costs at either a fixed or performance-based rate.

However, for some small or new businesses, this may be the only cost-effective way to get into the marketplace as setting up your own process to directly sell to customers can result in high start up costs with significant associated risk.

Build your Business Planning plan

Build your business plan by answering the questions below. A plan will automatically be generated, based on your responses.

Strategy

Q.1 How will you get the product/service to the end-user and what channel of distribution will you use?

Q.2 What systems will be implemented for processing orders, shipping and billing?

Competitive Strategies

Competitive strategies are the method by which you achieve a competitive advantage in the market.

There are, typically, three types of competitive strategies that can be implemented. They are:

- » cost leadership
- » differentiation
- » focus strategy.

A mixture of two or more of these strategies is also possible, depending on your business' objectives and current market position.

Cost leadership

The aim of this strategy is to be a low-cost producer relative to your competitors and is particularly useful in markets where price is a deciding factor. Cost leadership is often achieved by carefully selecting suppliers and production techniques to minimise production, distribution and marketing costs.

Be sure to be aware of any serious loss in quality that may render low-cost ineffective.

Differentiation

A differentiation strategy seeks to develop a competitive advantage through supplying and marketing a product that is in some way different to what the competition is doing.

If developed successfully, this strategy can potentially reduce price sensitivity and improve brand loyalty from customers.

Focus strategy

This strategy recognises that marketing to a homogenous customer group may not be an effective strategy for the product your business is selling. Instead, the business focuses its marketing efforts on different selected market segments.

That is, identify the needs, wants and interests of the particular market segments and customise marketing techniques to reflect those characteristics.

Advertising and Promotions

The main objective of advertising and promoting your products is to attract the attention of customers and, subsequently, persuade them to purchase form your business. It is a way of communicating the benefits of your products to your target audience.

Similar to other areas of successful business operation, advertising involves setting clear goals and objectives.

One of the benefits of advertising is that it gives you the opportunity to communicate a message to a large audience at one time - reducing the cost per contact. However, advertising can also be performed at a smaller and more specialised scale to target a specific market.

Obviously, small business isn't able to compete with large corporations in terms of their marketing budget, so cost-effective strategies are generally a good option in most cases.

Some cost-effective advertising solutions include:
- » Local Directories in both print and online.
- » Signage of vehicles, shop fronts, stationery and uniforms.
- » Displaying promotional material at community locations or at non-competitive businesses.
- » Advertising on the reverse side of receipts.
- » Radio, television and print advertisements.
- » Event sponsorship

If you have little knowledge of how to effectively manage the advertisement of your business, it may be a good idea to seek independent advice from someone such as an advertising agency.

While this may at first seem like an expensive option, it may be better than investing your entire advertising budget into a strategy that fails to achieve results for your business.

It is important to note that people who have been pleased by your customer service or product offering are likely to pass on good comments to others.

By managing good relations with your customers you are effectively using them to advertise your business through word-of-mouth.

Build your Business Planning plan

Build your business plan by answering the questions below. A plan will automatically be generated, based on your responses.

Strategy

Q.1 What is your advertising strategy, how does it support the desired positioning of your business?

Q.2 List and describe the forms of sales promotions you will use to help sell your product/service. Will this be seasonal?

Q.3 Why are these forms of sales promotions the most effective and how will they benefit your business?

Q.4 What is the total cost of all your sales promotional efforts?

Q.5 What is your strategy for achieving a positive image through public relations (PR)?

Q.6 Why is this the most effective method and what are the benefits for your business?

Q.7 Will you use external public relations agencies?

Q.8 How will you minimise potential negative PR?

Q.9 What is the total cost of all your PR activities?

Q.10 Will you have a website for your business? If so will you have just simple promotion on the site or offer other features such as online catalogues or online ordering?

Q.11 Who will be responsible for developing, maintaining and ensuring that the website is being utilised effectively? E.g. search engine optimisation and affiliate exchange programs.

Q.12 What is the total cost of training your sales staff?

Q.13 What training will be provided to assist staff in achieving sales objectives?

Q.14 How does your advertising and promotion strategy reinforce the customer benefits available through your unique selling proposition (USP)?

Q.15 How does your advertising and promotion strategy focus your promotion efforts and spend on your identified target market?

Q.16 List and describe the forms of advertising you will use to promote your product/service and the frequency of the advert?

Q.17 List and describe the forms of direct mail you will use to promote your product/service. Will this be seasonal?

Q.18 Why are these forms of direct mail the most effective and how will they benefit your business?

Q.19 What is the total cost of all your advertising efforts?

Q.20 What sales method will you use (brokers, commissioned salespersons, etc)?

Q.21 Why is this the most effective selling process, how will it benefit your business?

Q.22 What tools will be provided to salespersons to assist in achieving sales?

Q.23 Will you be offering incentives to salespersons for achieving set goals? If so, describe.

Q.24 What is the total planned cost of your online marketing efforts?

Operating Plan

This chapter outlines building a basic operating plan to help set up and begin running your business. It includes information on staffing, systems and processes, equipment, facilities and general risk management.

People

There are many points that require consideration when employing people to assist with the operation of your business. These relate to the hiring of staff, your legal obligations to employees, staff management and the termination of employment.

When hiring new staff, you will need to consider:

- » Type/Number of employees
- » Hidden costs of employment
- » Employee roles and responsibilities
- » Employee skills, attributes and experience
- » Recruitment costs, time and resources

You will also need to make yourself aware of your legal obligations as an employer including:

- » Occupational Health and Safety regulations
- » Workers Compensation cover
- » Employee Superannuation
- » Equal Employment Opportunity and anti-discrimination legislation
- » Wages and leave entitlements
- » Taxation obligations and records/reporting

It is also important to be able to manage and retain your

employees. In order to effectively do this you should consider:

- » Employee induction, training and development
- » Policies and procedures to reduce and deal with complaints, disputes and employee relations
- » Reviews, feedback and incentives, in regards to employee performance

At some stage you may be faced with ending a staff member's employment.

Therefore, it is important to have thought about the following:

- » Policies and procedures for ending employment through either resignation, redundancy or dismissal
- » Employer obligations to employees who have resigned, been made redundant or dismissed

Effectively managing the people within your business is fundamental to its success.

It is important to be able to find, recruit, develop and retain good employees. By doing so, you can ensure that your employees understand the objectives of the business and work towards business development and customer satisfaction.

Build your Business Planning plan

Build your business plan by answering the questions below. A plan will automatically be generated based on your responses.

Operating Plan

Q.1 How many employees will you have?

Q.2 What are their job descriptions?

Q.3 What are your projections in regards to staff turnover?

BUSINESS PLANNING

Q.4 What are your plans in regards to training and development of your employees?

Q.5 What are some of the potential risks that may arise in relation to staff?

Q.6 What measures will you implement to reduce the impact of these risks?

Q.7 Are you aware of your obligations to your employees, in terms of entitlements?

Systems & Processes

Planning and designing systems and processes for business operations involves the arrangement of management and staff, their roles and functions and business administration requirements.

It also takes into account business facilities and equipment, inventory management as well as policies and procedures for other business functions.

To plan business systems effectively, you can utilise the following planning process:

- » Analyse the Business Situation: this involves taking into consideration the current business environment and the costs and benefits of implementing a new system.
- » Establish the System Purpose and Goals: define the purpose of the new system and what you expect to achieve from it. This could be for example, to improve staff productivity when making a sale.
- » Assign Responsibility and Milestones: assign responsibility for implementing the strategy to individual employees, with a timeline to achieve the identified goals.
- » Communicate the Strategy and Plan to Employees: ensure that employees understand what is required of them and the direction that they follow.

» Acknowledge Achievement of Goals: when goals and objectives are met, offer some form of reward as an incentive to encourage and thank people for their efforts.

Build your Business Planning plan

Build your business plan by answering the questions below. A plan will automatically be generated based on your responses. Avoid changing your answers offline, as they will not be saved to your profile.

Operating Plan

Q.1 What systems or processes will you implement in relation to the management of your staff?

Q.2 What is the total cost of all your equipment?

Q.3 To what extent will your operations be automated?

Q.4 Is this the most effective option for your business and why?

Q.5 What is the total cost for achieving your desired level of automation?

Q.6 How do you plan on achieving and managing quality in your operations?

Q.7 What does this mean in terms of costs to your business?

Q.8 What steps will you take or what strategies will you implement to minimise defects in your products/services?

Q.9 How do you plan on dealing with defects if and when they arise?

Q.10 What system will you have in place to manage your inventory?

Q.11 What does this mean in terms of costs to your business?

Q.12 How will this system add value to your business?

Q.13 Assess the maximum operating capacity of your

business.

Q.14 How do you plan on dealing with inefficient parts of your business i.e. that may not operate at their full capacity?

Q.15 Describe your current capacity strategy and how does it line up with your operational goals?

Q.16 If you are required to expand your operational capacity, what factors will you consider while taking this decision and why?

Q.17 What steps will you take or what strategies will you implement to minimise process constraints in your operations?

Q.18 How do you plan on dealing with process constraints if and when they arise?

Q.19 Describe the types of equipment you will be using. Will it be general-purpose or special-purpose equipment?

Q.20 What is the total cost of all your employees?

Q.21 Will you be having a flexible workforce i.e. employees that are capable of doing many tasks? If so, why have you chosen this option and what advantages will it provide to your business?

Q.22 What system will you have in place to recognise and reward employees for achieving business goals and objectives?

Q.23 What systems and procedures will you have in place to ensure quality control?

Q.24 How will this process structure add value to your operation?

Q.25 Will operations management be a core focus for your business? If so, how will you go about achieving this?

Q.26 Will you be hiring an operations manager or will you be undertaking this role yourself?

Q.27 Will there be an emphasis on good project management within your business? If so, how will you go about achieving this?

Q.28 How will you approach undertaking a new project? I.e. do you plan on hiring new project team members to suit the demands of a new project or will you only be taking on projects that will only require your existing team's capabilities?

Q.29 What are some of the tools you will use to monitor projects? i.e. Gantt charts

Q.30 Will you be conducting any risk assessments before commencing a project? If so, how?

Q.31 What are your competitive priorities?

Q.32 Describe your process strategies and how they line up with your competitive priorities?

Q.33 Why are these the most effective strategies and how will they add value to your operation?

Q.34 Describe the process structure of your operation and how you plan on managing it.

Q.35 Why did you select this structure and have you considered other alternatives?

Q.36 To what extent will customers be involved in your business from an operational point of view?

Q.37 Taking into consideration the efficiency of your operations, what are some of the potential difficulties that may arise from customer involvement?

Q.38 Alternatively, what are some of the potential advantages of having your customers involved in your operations?

Q.39 What does this mean in terms of costs to your business?

Equipment

To ensure a smooth and effective business operations startup, it is important to have the right equipment in place at the outset. This includes not only production equipment but administration and communication equipment. After determining the equipment you require, you will also need to finance the costs.

The equipment you require for your business to become fully operational is dependent on your particular situation.

Some small business owners will find that they require very little in terms of equipment or use equipment that need only be purchased once at the initial start up stage. Other organisations need more substantial equipment, such as in a production company, with higher initial costs, as well as ongoing maintenance and upgrading expenses.

There are a number of methods that you can use to finance the initial acquisition of equipment. Depending on your circumstances, you may seek finance from friends or relatives, your own personal savings or loans from financial institutions. It may also be possible to secure credit from your suppliers or lease equipment on a periodic basis.

Build your Business Planning plan

Build your business plan by answering the questions below. A plan will automatically be generated, based on your responses.

Operating Plan

Q.1 List and describe any vehicle, plant, and equipment requirements of your business.

Facilities

Choosing business premises requires careful planning and consideration. An inappropriate or poor location can be damaging to your business, particularly where the business relies on ease of access or exposure to consumers.

In order to make an informed decision when selecting a facility from which to conduct business, you should keep in mind the needs of your employees, customers and general operations.

Facility Requirements
- » Does your business have any special needs such as low noise levels, space for equipment, storage, parking, etc?
- » What type of space do you require in order to effectively interact with your customers?
- » Is there any competition or other businesses in the area that could cause problems or difficulties with your operations?
- » Are the premises large enough for what the business needs both now and into the future?

Costs
- » How much can the business afford to spend?
- » Will the location cost customers any money (parking, etc.)?
- » Consider land tax expenses.
- » How will the cost of the facility impact business profitability and product pricing?
- » Does the facility require any costly alterations?

Convenience:
- » Can customers find, travel to and access the business easily?
- » Is their enough exposure to attract customers (traffic, pedestrians, etc)?
- » Availability of parking.
- » Do your clients have any special needs (disabilities, etc)?
- » How secure and safe is the area?

There are a number of different types of facilities available for businesses to operate from, with each suiting different circumstances.

A commercial lease provides you with the right to occupy the premises for a fee, however you will need to consider the terms of the lease agreement before entering into it.

It may also be possible in some cases to work from home which is convenient but can come with distractions. A business may also choose to purchase a building outright if the plan is to conduct operations from the location for an extended period of time.

Build your Business Planning plan

Build your business plan by answering the questions below. A plan will automatically be generated based on your responses.

Operating Plan

Q.1 What type of facilities does your business require?

Q.2 Will you require any special alterations to suit your business needs?

Managing Risks

Risk management involves identifying unfavourable events that could negatively affect your business if they happen to occur and developing strategies to overcome them.

Risk events that could potentially occur range from minor to serious and likely to unlikely. This range includes:

- » Natural Disaster
- » Key business staff leaving
- » Key suppliers relocating or closing down, or a change in their credit policies
- » Litigation

- Poor cash flow
- Family emergency
- A breakdown in occupational health and safety
- Bad debts

There are four key strategies that you can implement to cope with business risk:

- Risk Prevention: guards are put in place to stop or deter the risk from ever happening. This may include putting guards on production equipment to prevent common workplace accidents or security locks and alarms on your business premises.
- Risk Avoidance: this involves developing strategies or not undertaking activities so that the business would not have to face the risk. An example is not entering into a contract to avoid facing a particular liability.
- Risk Retention: this is when you accept that a risk event may occur and taking no action to prevent, avoid or stop it from happening. You plan to deal with the problem when it actually occurs.
- Risk Transfer: in some cases you can transfer the risk of an event happening onto others, usually in the form of a contract. Examples include taking out insurance and selling your outstanding debtor accounts to a debt collection agency.
- Conducting a risk analysis can also be a good risk reduction technique.

This involves identifying a risk, determining its probability of occurring and developing strategies to overcome the risk, if any. There are a number of available worksheets and explanations available online to assist you in performing a risk analysis and development of a risk-management plan.

Build your Business Planning plan

Build your business plan by answering the questions below. A plan will automatically be generated based on your responses.

Operating Plan

Q.1 What are some of the potential risk factors that could adverse effects on the operation of your business?

Q.2 How will you prevent or minimise the effects of these risks?

Management Team

This chapter examines the issues to consider when selecting a management team, used to help run and manage your business. This includes identifying key roles, developing job descriptions and defining your organisation structure with an organisational chart.

Key Personnel

If your organisation is of a size that requires key business roles to be delegated to management staff, it is critically important to ensure you have a suitable management structure in place. You need to select suitably qualified and experienced personnel to fill the roles.

To help you plan and develop a management structure and select the best people for each position, you can create a list of all of the tasks that need to be performed to run the business and the responsibilities involved for each function such as supervision of employees.

You can then establish key management positions and assign roles and responsibilities to each position. This will help you to match up suitable personnel to each key management function.

Once you have defined the key management positions

and their relevant requirements, you can develop this into a "job description" document.

Job descriptions provide the opportunity to clearly communicate each individual's roles and responsibilities and also serve as a way to measure performance by setting Key Performance Indicators (KPIs).

A job description generally includes the following:

- » Duties/tasks to be performed
- » Responsibilities within the business
- » Working conditions
- » Material and equipment the employee is required to operate
- » Working relationships, teamwork and individual work
- » Reporting relationships
- » Relevant performance indicators and measurement details
- » Other relevant job relevant information as suitable
- » Organisational Structure

With the necessary functions needed to run the business and the roles of key individuals in the organisation defined, you can develop and refine the structure by producing an organisational chart.

This chart is a tool that helps to define the inter-relationships between all departments, divisions, teams and people. It defines reporting structures and lines of authority and responsibility, providing a picture of how the organisation functions.

Failing to define workplace roles and lines of authority can create tension, miscommunication and inefficiency within your business. People may be unsure as to what jobs are their own and who they are required to report to creating inefficiencies that can cost time and money.

Usually business organisational structures are planned as a

hierarchy with the most senior position in the business (usually the owner) at the top and those with the least authority within the business on the bottom.

Organisational hierarchies have become flatter in the past decade to promote better communication and more employee responsibility within the workplace.

This means that a lower ranked employee is able to communicate directly with those above him without necessarily having to go through middle management where ideas or complaints may be disregarded.

Build your Business Planning plan

Build your business plan by answering the questions below. A plan will automatically be generated based on your responses.

Operating Plan

Q.1 Provide an overview of your business' organisational structure.

Q.2 How will you ensure that your employees understand this organisational structure?

Motivating Employees

In order to find, retain and manage the people with the right skills for your business, you need to consider what employees may be looking for in a job. There are a number of motivators besides money that people are interested in.

As an employer you can offer performance incentives as a way of motivating your staff. Incentives are rewards for achieving goals. Employers can set out an incentive early on and reward employees when they meet or exceed a certain goal, objective or deadline. The idea is that as the employee achieves more highly and the business also succeeds meaning a win-win situation for both employee and employer.

Another way to motivate your staff is by offering an improved work-life balance. Work-life balance refers to adjusting work patterns to assist employees in combining work with their other responsibilities, such as family and community commitments. This may include working part-time, job-sharing, flexible rosters or even working from home.

You may also consider providing a certain amount of unpaid leave for when it is required. This allows people to stay in the workforce in situations where they may otherwise have had to leave.

A better work-life balance may also help to reduce employee stress, improve productivity and decrease unscheduled absenteeism.

All of these factors can reduce staff turnover and improve loyalty and commitment.

Financial Planning

This chapter outlines financing and budgeting considerations for small businesses including sources of government funding and support as well as a summary of different types of financial statements.

Assets

Assets are items that your business owns, which have commercial value and help to generate revenue for your business. Assets may be tangible in that they have physical characteristics, such as inventory or office equipment, or they can be intangible assets without physical existence, such as copyrights, patents or research and development.

Assets are classified into two categories:

» Current assets: cash or other assets that would normally be consumed or converted into cash within

twelve months, such as accounts receivable and inventory.
» Non-current assets: all assets that would not be consumed or converted into cash within twelve months, including land, buildings and equipment.

As most assets lose value over time through obsolescence, age or wear and tear they can also be reduced from an accounting point of view which is called depreciation. Depreciation is a non cash expense which accounts for the reduction in value of the asset over its useful life. Depreciation also has the effect of lowering the company's reported earnings.

When calculating asset depreciation there are four factors that need to be taken into account:

» The cost of the asset, including all necessary costs to bring the asset into use such as shipping and installation costs.
» The asset's anticipated useful life.
» The estimated residual value of the asset at the end of its useful life.
» The method of calculating depreciation:
» Straight Line Method
» Units of Production based depreciation
» Accelerated Depreciation

The straight line method is the most common depreciation method for small business as it is the simplest to use. This method allocates the amount to be depreciated evenly over the useful life of the asset.

It can be calculated as follows:

Straight Line Depreciation = (Cost - Residual value) ÷ Useful life

Liabilities & Equity

Liabilities are any existing obligations that the business has to its creditors, which will ultimately result in the outflow of assets or cash to another entity.

Liabilities are classified into two categories:
- » Current liabilities are liabilities are due and payable within twelve months. These include accounts payable, wages and rent.
- » Non-current liabilities are liabilities that are due and payable in a period over twelve months. An example is long-term loans such as mortgage repayments.

Equity is what is left after deducting all the business' liabilities from its total assets. It is classified into two categories:
- » Capital contributions are made by business owners. It is important to note that creditor's claims to your business' assets take legal precedence over business owners. Hence, business owners take the ultimate risk when investing in the business.
- » Retained earnings are from the business' previous profitable periods of operation. Start-up businesses don't have this during their first year of operation.

Build your Business Planning plan

Build your business plan by answering the questions below. A plan will automatically be generated, based on your responses.

Financial Plan

Q.1 Identify all assumptions regarding your liabilities and equity when preparing your business' projected financial statements.

Assessing your Requirements

When starting a business, one of the first and most critical points to address is identifying all the potential costs you will face. These include both the start-up costs and the ongoing costs.

Start-up costs are the initial outlays when setting up your business. These are one-off costs that occur before your business begins trading. Typical start-up costs include shop fit-outs, factory and office setup, equipment and machinery purchases, office supplies, business and other registrations, licence and permit fees, along with any legal costs.

Ongoing costs are the recurring costs necessary to run and maintain the business. These costs include items such as wages and on-costs, mortgage/rent, electricity expenses, insurance and advertising costs.

It is also very important to consider including an allowance or "float" as working capital for the early stages where you may not necessarily be generating enough revenue to cover all your costs.

Once you have obtained this information, you will be able to prepare a detailed budget that covers the start-up costs, ongoing costs and initial working capital requirements so you can calculate your overall financing requirements.

Build your Business Planning plan

Build your business plan by answering the questions below. A plan will automatically be generated based on your responses.

Financial Plan

Q.1 Develop a realistic start-up budget for your business.

Types of Financing

There are two main sources of finance:

» Equity Financing - money invested into your business in exchange for a share in its ownership.

- » Debt Financing - usually in the form of a loan where the principal amount borrowed and interest accumulated on the loan needs to be paid.

There are a number of sources of equity finance available to business.

This includes:

- » Personal Savings: money that you personally invest into the business.
- » Friends and Relatives: people that you personally know invest into the business to lend assistance.
- » Angel Investors: wealthy individuals who lend their personal finances to a business in return for a share in its ownership.
- » Venture Capital: applications to professionally managed third parties such as a superannuation fund who lend finance based on a good business plan.

There are also a range of opportunities to secure debt financing such as:

- » Leasing: hiring out equipment for a regular fee for the duration of the lease term, with no outlay to actually purchase equipment.
- » Term Loans: paid back to a financial institution over an agreed period.
- » Credit Cards: easy to acquire financial institution loans that carry high interest rates.
- » Bank Overdrafts: where you withdraw more than your account contains, with interest calculated on your outstanding balance.
- » Commercial Bills: short-term loans where the amount must be paid in full upon reaching expiry.

- » Loan Programs: short-term loans set up to assist small business with initial start up expenses.
- » Trade Credit: deferred payment of goods and services purchased from a supplier.

Build your Business Planning plan

Build your business plan by answering the questions below. A plan will automatically be generated, based on your responses.

Financial Plan

Q.1 Identify your key financial objectives.

Government Funding & Assistance

Government grants and assistance are available for those wanting to start a business and those already in business. These grants are made available to encourage people who may not have the funds to start their own business.

They also help to stimulate economic growth and business development around the country.

There is an emphasis on giving people wanting to start their own innovative business venture an opportunity to do so. Funding and programs can come from federal, state and territory levels of government and, in some instances, from local councils.

There are usually grants available for people from low socio-economic backgrounds, young people, innovative businesses, etc.

Obtaining Finance

To maximise the chances of your financing application being successful it is important that you carefully plan your application and get well prepared to answer questions about your business and yourself.

Traditionally bankers look at the four criteria when assessing the risks associated with lending you money:

- » Character - involves collecting personal details about who you are. It includes details about your business skills, professionalism, you knowledge and experience within the industry, and your ability to manage a business.
- » Credit - involves collecting details about your credit history
- » Collateral - involves determining the assets that can be used as security for your loan.
- » Cash flow - Your ability to pay back the loan

A well prepared business plan and a collection of your personal information regarding these criteria can significantly support your loan application as it demonstrates the amount of thought you have put into your business.

To further contribute to the application of your loan you should have information about the following:

- » Finance Required: Determine how much you require to start the operation of your business. Consider in your calculation amounts for operating costs for the first few months of business operation, equipment purchases and business start-up.
- » Business Type: This entails describing your business and providing details about the market you will be selling too, associated market research, pricing structures, business goals as well as proposed products and services your business is going to sell.
- » History: When raising debt financing you need to ensure you address your past character (previous experience, skills, etc), credit history and any collateral you possess.

- » Usage of Finance: This involves justifying the amount of investment your business requires. To do this, you should project budgets into the coming years, prepare cash flow statements and profit and loss statements as well as a list of current and intended creditors.
- » Finance Repayment: This involves clearly establishing how the investment will be repaid, in what timeframe and to what conditions. A list of personal assets that could be used as security for the loan should also be included.

Build your Business Planning plan

Build your business plan by answering the questions below. A plan will automatically be generated, based on your responses.

Financial Plan

Q.1 Assess the various sources of financing available for starting up your business.

Profit & Loss Statement

A Profit and Loss Statement (also known as an Income Statement or a Statement of Financial Performance), communicates the profitability of your business in a particular financial period.

The profit and loss statement consists of three main elements:

- » Income: Represents all inflows of economic benefits into your business. It consists of revenue and gains. Revenue is the inflows that result from general business activities and investments, such as sales or interest received. Gains are inflows that result from the sale of business assets.

- » Cost of Goods Sold: The total cost of inventory that is sold during the period.
- » Expenses: Effectively, this is all business outgoings incurred during the period, other than the distribution of income or assets to the owners of the business. Examples include sales and distribution expenses, business administration expenses, and financing expenses such as interest paid to business creditors.

In brief, the profit and loss statement is calculated as follows:

Net profit = (Revenue - COGS) Gains – Expenses

If income exceeds expenses the business will have made a profit. On the other hand, if expenses exceed income, the business would have suffered a loss for the period.

Build your Business Planning plan

Build your business plan by answering the questions below. A plan will automatically be generated based on your responses.

Financial Plan

Q.1 Prepare a 12-month and 5-year profit and loss statement for your business.

Balance Sheet

The balance sheet (also known as the Statement for Financial Position), provides you with the "net worth" of your business' assets and liabilities at a certain date. It is useful when evaluating the efficiency of your business in using its financial resources for operating purposes.

To summarise how a balance sheet is calculated is the accounting equation:

Equity = Assets - Liabilities

The balance sheet consists of the following three main elements:

» Assets: Assets are items that your business owns with commercial value. For example, business equipment, bank accounts or inventory.
» Accumulated Depreciation: is used as a contra-asset account to non-current assets. It reflects the amount consumed of a non-current asset to date.
» Liabilities: A liability is any existing obligation the business has to its creditors.

Assets and liabilities can be further classified into current and non-current.

As a rule of thumb, current means those assets and liabilities held for less than 12 months, and non-current are those assets and liabilities held by the business for over a 12 month period. However, this may change to suit your business's business cycle.

Equity is the leftover amount after deducting all the business' creditors' claims in the forms of liabilities to business assets from total assets. The business creditor's claims to your business' assets take legal precedence over business owners' claims.

Build your Business Planning plan

Build your business plan by answering the questions below. A plan will automatically be generated based on your responses.

Financial Plan

Q.1 Prepare a 12-month and 5-year balance sheet for your business. To ensure accuracy and consistency, the figures should be taken from your profit and loss statements.

Cash Flow Statement

A cash flow statement represents the cash inflows and outflows from the business' activities for the reporting period.

Cash inflows are all the cash the business receives during the period and cash outflows are all the cash the business expends during the period.

The cash flow statement communicates important information regarding the businesses including:

- » Ability to pay creditors on time
- » Ability to receive cash from debtors on time
- » Ability of the business to generate a positive cash flow (where cash inflows exceed cash outflows)
- » To establish the business's need for external financing.

When the closing balance figure is negative this means that there is a negative cash flow, with cash outflows exceeding the inflow of cash into the business.

Build your Business Planning plan

Build your business plan by answering the questions below. A plan will automatically be generated based on your responses.

Financial Plan

Q.1 Prepare a 12-month and 5-year cash flow statement for your business. To ensure accuracy and consistency, the figures should be taken from your profit and loss statements and balance sheets.

Budgeting

Budgets are used as a planning tool to plan and predict future income inflows and expenditures. They are also used to benchmark performance as a point of comparison between expected and actual income and expenditure.

Budgets should also be used when applying for financing using various projection periods. Budgets are also used to represent what you plan to use the financing on in order to maximise your business' success and generate a positive net income.

To budget you must first determine your business start-up costs and the business operating costs for the initial years of operating.

You should maintain some slack in your business budget to accommodate any unforeseen spending such as when an emergency or a good opportunity arises. It is important, however, not to be too optimistic when budgeting; be realistic, particularly in respect of business sales.

There are many types of budgets available to operate a business, including the three key budgets outlined below:

- » Projected Income Statement: This employs the profit and loss statement where you budget for total business sales and expenses for the projection period.
- » Projected Balance Sheet: This budget employs the balance sheet to project the business' assets it needs to operate and the amount of liabilities the business expects to incur during the period, including creditor claims.
- » Cash Flow Budget: This employs the cash flow statement to enable you to plan and represent your expected cash inflows and outflows.

Action Plan

This chapter is designed to assist you in understanding what an Action Plan is, how to develop one, and how it will help your business to achieve short and long-term business goals.

What is an Action Plan?

An action plan integrates all of the strategies you have developed throughout your business plan into a highly organised and prioritised plan of action designed to achieve your stated business mission and goals.

This is achieved by breaking down the strategies you developed into small, achievable steps and then identifying the actions you need to take for each step. It can be used as a short-term (6-12 months) action plan to achieve short-term business goals, a medium-term action plan (2-3 years) or a long-term action plan (3-5 years).

An action plan identifies the business goal (what you would like to achieve) and the strategies that can be implemented to reach that goal.

It also explains the specific actions that need to take place in order to achieve the business strategy.

This will include the timeframe, roles and responsibilities, performance indicators and alternative methods that can be implemented to reach the business objectives.

Developing an Action Plan

Generally action plans are limited to a small and manageable number of goals. This helps to keep the plan realistic and achievable.

For each action you should identify:

» The timeframe and priorities for each action.
» The people who will be responsible for undertaking each action.
» Specific performance indicators to help you determine in the future whether your business has succeeded in achieving the business goal.

Once you have these details identified, you can progress to formulating a series of strategies to be undertaken to achieve the goals of each action item. It often helps to break the various strategies tasks down into simple and specific steps to keep the plan on track and avoid getting overwhelmed or losing control.

An important step is being able to evaluate within a set period of time if the action plan has been a success. Failing to do so could result in a plan that continues on indefinitely without ever actually achieving anything positive for the business.

To evaluate your action plan, go back to the initial objectives you set out and decide if they have worked, not worked or are in the process of being achieved. Be critical of each objectives success or failure in this stage. If your original targets were too optimistic, then you need to admit this so that you will be able to move on.

Sometimes it may become apparent that an action plan has failed to meet its objectives. Therefore, you may need to reassess and redefine your original objectives and strategies to improve their success or abandon the plan and start again at the beginning rather than waste resources on a plan that isn't working.

Build your Business Planning plan

Build your business plan by answering the questions below. A plan will automatically be generated based on your responses.

Implementation

Q.1 Develop an action plan which outlines the key tasks and activities required to implement your business plan.

NOTES

www.CEO-OnDemand.com.au
www.MoreProfitLessTime.com

2 MARKETING AND SALES

What is Marketing?

This chapter assists you in understanding the basic concept of marketing, the competitive strategies that you could adopt in your marketing process as well as the importance of defining your marketing objective.

It also guides you in developing your unique selling proposition as well as developing marketing strategies for business and consumer markets.

Marketing Philosophy

The purpose of marketing is to gain a balance between creating more value for customers against making profits for the organisation. To achieve this, many firms have adopted a marketing philosophy or what is generally termed a "marketing orientation".

A marketing orientation can be defined as focusing the organisation on identifying and understanding the customers' preferences in terms of needs and wants and delivering them more effectively and efficiently than competitors.

Prior to the adoption of a marketing orientation, many organisations followed what was referred to as the "Production Philosophy". This approach focused on improving the efficiency of production and distribution to reduce costs and deliver more affordable products as the source of competitive advantage.

Another philosophy that has been followed historically is the "Selling Concept". This approach required organisations to aggressively focus on selling and promotion efforts as a way to stimulate demand and drive sales.

A marketing-driven approach or marketing orientation has consistently delivered superior results over these other philosophies. Adopting a marketing orientation is now widely accepted as delivering greater levels of customer satisfaction, profitability and sustainability.

Competitive Strategies

Most successful organisations develop strategies to deal with their particular environment that offers the company the strongest possible competitive advantage.

In developing these strategies, questions that are commonly addressed include the following;

- » Should we compete?
- » If so, which markets should we compete in?
- » How should we compete?

As all business situations are different, there is no one strategy that is a best fit for all companies. However, there are three types of competitive strategies that you could adopt depending on your position in the market and particular objectives:

Overall cost leadership

Organisations that follow this strategy aim to win a large market share by achieving the lowest cost of production and distribution to offer lower prices than competitors. "Aldi" supermarkets are viewed as an organisation that follows a cost leadership, with its approach to offer a limited number of quality products at low prices.

Its emphasis is on minimising costs at all levels in the value chain, and is proven through its business philosophy, "top quality at incredibly low prices".

Differentiation

This strategy leads the organisation to concentrate on creating a highly differentiated product line and marketing program in order to become the class leader in the industry. Woolworths' supermarket business, with its theme 'the fresh food people' has been particularly successful with its differentiation strategy, by positioning the business around the primary value of 'fresh', which is highly regarded by a large proportion of supermarket buyers.

Focus/Niche

Organisations that follow this strategy are usually smaller firms that focus efforts on serving a few market segments effectively rather than dealing with the whole market.

A company could either use a cost focus, which aims at becoming a low-cost producer for a niche segment or a differentiation focus which aims at differentiated products in the niche segment.

Small delis that focus on a smaller market proportion can be identified as organisations that follow this strategy.

In summary, it is important to pursue a clear strategy in order to succeed. Firms that do not pursue a clear strategy also known as the 'middle-of-the-roaders', often find it difficult to compete and establish a clear position and competitive advantage in the market.

Marketing Objectives

Marketing objectives define what you want to accomplish through your marketing activities. There are several important factors to consider when establishing effective marketing objectives.

SMART Approach = Setting specific, Measurable, Achievable, Realistic and Time-specific objectives

When setting objectives, it is very important to ensure that your objectives are; specific, measurable, achievable, realistic and time specific, or SMART for short.

The "SMART" approach allows you to effectively manage your marketing activities and importantly be able to determine how successful they have been and whether they have delivered the particular benefits sought.

The "SMART" approach is explained to illustrate how you address each area;

- » **Specific** - are your objectives stated in a way that is precise about what you are hoping to achieve?
- » **Measurable** - Can you quantify each objective, i.e. can you use a unit of measure, such as market share in percentage or dollars, or other, to provide a way to check your level of success?
- » **Achievable** - Are your objectives reasonable in terms of what you can actually achieve or are you setting your sights too high?
- » **Realistic** - Do you have sufficient employees and resources to achieve the objectives you have set? If you don't then they are likely to be unrealistic.
- » **Time specific** - When are you hoping to achieve these objectives? You need to define a timing plan with target timing for each specific objective.

As an example, ABC stationery supplier sells its goods

to newsagents across the country and they want to boost revenue for their product range. To detail this objective more clearly, we could define it using the "SMART" approach as follows:

To gain 30% market share for stationery by December 31, 2015.

- » Specific - need to understand the latest preferences of customers in the identified segments and appropriately target each stationery item such as pens, exercise books, rulers, and calculators to maximise sales volumes
- » Measurable - current market share is 20%, will set a target of 30% market share, meaning we need an extra 10%, market share amounts can be established based by monitoring the overall value of sales in terms of dollars
- » Achievable - ensuring technical competency and commitment of all personnel involved in the development and implementation of strategy. This can range from having an experienced and knowledgeable marketing team to capable sales staff. Access to funding is also necessary for the acquisition of extra stock to fulfil increased demand.
- » Realistic - the objective is realistic as the marketing resources are in place to conduct the segmenting and targeting exercise and access to the extra stock required.
- » Time-Specific - the increase in market share is to be achieved within 12 months, a regular progress update will be taken every month to track level of success.

Linking marketing objectives to strategies

Your marketing objectives should also be consistent and indicate the priorities of the organisation. This means that objectives should flow from the mission statement of your business, towards the financial objectives and to the rest of the marketing plan.

For example, ABC Garden Centre has, as part of its strategic plan, a goal to grow the business by diversifying its product range, with the specific financial objective of achieving a 10% growth in overall sales, which means an extra $75,000 in revenue.

A linked marketing objective could be to add pre-packaged garden soil as a new complementary product line to be offered with plant sales. To grow the business as per the strategic goal and meet the financial objective of $75,000 in extra sales, it has been calculated that a total of 7,500 bags will need to be sold at their selling price of $10 each.

Provide direction to employees

Clearly defined objectives may also provide direction for your employees in terms of what to achieve and in what period. They also serve as motivators for your employees by creating an attainable challenge that they can strive to achieve.

Build your Marketing plan

Build your business plan by answering the questions below. A plan will automatically be generated based on your responses.

Marketing Objectives

Q.1 What are your marketing objectives in terms of revenue?

Q.2 What are your marketing objectives in terms of your market share?

Q.3 What are your marketing objectives in terms of your product/service?

Unique Selling Proposition (USP)

The starting point in developing your marketing strategy is to come up with your unique selling proposition (USP). A USP is what makes your product or service stand out from your competitors and is generally the reason why customers will purchase your product or service over those of your competitors.

Some of the common USPs are 'best service', 'lowest price', 'best value', and 'most advanced technology'. The aim is to identify these factors and convey them in the marketplace. To convey your USP to customers, you can consider developing it as a tagline to go with your logo if you have one and printing it on all your marketing communications such as business cards, letter heads, brochures, web site etc.

Consider Intel's USP; in order to be in line with Cyrix's fast computer chips, Intel launched its 'Intel Inside' campaign which aimed at awarding all manufacturers and dealers of computers an advertising allowance to include the 'Intel inside' symbol. Through the co-branded advertising with its business customers, the 'Intel Inside' logo became very popular among the final consumers.

This well created unique selling proposition has increased sales and rewarded Intel with large profits.

Some other examples of famous taglines are following;

- » Canon - Advanced Simplicity
- » Nike - Just Do It!
- » MasterCard - There are some things money can't buy
- » Honda - The Power of Dreams
- » Microsoft - Where Do You Want to Go Today; Your Potential, Our Passion
- » HSBC - The World's Local Bank
- » BMW - The Ultimate Driving Machine

In order to maximise the overall benefit from your USP, ensure that you also communicate it to your staff so that they can understand what it is and why it exists, then feel a sense of ownership and commitment to it.

Adding Value to your products

Adding value to your product or service is an important point to consider when developing a USP. Value-adding is when organisations provide their customers a product or service that is over and above the core product / service.

The value-added component is therefore not necessarily expected by the customer, but when supplied with the purchase provides additional benefit and a potential source of differentiation from competitors.

An example of value-adding can be things like extended product warranties, free delivery, or bonus product features.

Build your Marketing plan

Build your business plan by answering the questions below. A plan will automatically be generated, based on your responses.

Product/Service Overview

Q.1 What is your product's unique selling proposition? i.e. what makes your product different from your competitors?

Business vs Consumer Markets

The success of your marketing strategy involves gaining a comprehensive understanding of the particular markets that you serve. These markets can either be consumer markets or business markets.

A simple method of identifying the difference between these two markets is to address the following questions:

» Who is buying the goods?

» Why is the purchase being made?

Business markets involve sales and purchases of goods and services to various businesses, governments and market intermediaries to facilitate the finished product, which is generally then re-sold to an end user. In contrast, consumer markets involve the purchase and sale of goods and services to consumers for their own use rather than for resale.

As there is a significant difference between these two markets, the marketing strategies adopted to serve them also differ. These strategies need to be developed based on the needs, wants and buying processes of the particular market.

Buying decisions for consumer markets can be complex for large purchases such as cars, houses and holidays, where multiple family members such as husbands and wives, even children will be involved to make a collective decision. However, for smaller day-to-day products and services, there is usually a much simpler buying process, where one person will be the decision-maker and there will be generally a low-level relationship between the buyer and the seller, as in the case of a supermarket purchase.

In business markets however, the buying process may involve a high amount of decision-making and will often have more than one individual involved in the buying process. For example, there may be an engineer or technical person involved in the specification of the product or service and a purchasing manager in charge of price negotiations. Sometimes, in large buying decisions there can even be a team of people from different departments making the purchase decision collectively.

Build your Marketing plan

Build your business plan by answering the questions below. A plan will automatically be generated, based on your

responses.

Market Analysis

Q.1 Will you be targeting a business market, consumer market, or both?

Understanding your Market

This chapter assists you in understanding your market by focusing on identifying your consumers, competitors and the external factors that influence your business. It also guides you in conducting market research, identifying trends and conducting a SWOT analysis in order to identify your points of difference and points of parity.

Identifying Customers

Your market may consist of different customers with different buying behaviours. Some may prefer impulse purchasing while others may prefer taking their time and getting assistance from others. Getting a good understanding of how consumers think, what their buying habits are and what factors influence these habits is essential for you to make the most of your marketing opportunities.

There are six questions that are commonly asked in regard to consumer buying behavior:

» Why do consumers buy? Why will they buy the products or services on offer?
» Who buys? What are the characteristics of consumers that are likely to buy from you?
» What do they buy? Which products or services do they typically choose? What brands do they prefer?
» How do they buy? What are their buying habits? Do they buy because it is convenient or do they buy because it is easily accessible? Do they pay cash, or do they use credit cards?

- » Where do they buy? Do customers prefer to buy from mail order, retail stores, the internet or from door-to-door? How far are they prepared to travel to buy?
- » When do they buy? How much is the behaviour of customers affected by seasonal influences? What about the holiday season? How does that affect their shopping patterns? What about inflation or recession, or higher interest rates?

Influences on consumer behavior

There are many factors that can influence consumer buying behaviour. These can include personal factors; such as age and gender, social factors; such as social groups and culture, and psychological factors; such as personality and attitudes.

Social groups may be made up of family, friends, social clubs or sporting teams.

Each group develops its own set of normal behaviour and attitudes, which can dictate their buying habits. For example, surfers tend to wear certain types and brands of clothing, while younger children are interested in toys or the latest craze, such as skateboards or scooters.

Roles in the buying process

Identifying the roles in the buying process can help your organisation in developing the most effective marketing strategy for your business. Different people have different roles in the purchasing process of a particular product. For instance, if you consider a family, there can be different roles occupied by various family members as follows;

- » The person who suggests the idea of buying a particular product or service

- » The person who advises or carries some weight in making the final buying decision
- » The actual decision-maker who would ultimately make the buying decision
- » The person who would make the purchase
- » The user of the product. Therefore a company needs to identify who occupies which role or roles and thereby tailor the marketing strategy to suit.

Knowing the main participants and their roles in the buying process can help you to fine-tune the marketing strategy.

Build your Marketing plan

Build your business plan by answering the questions below. A plan will automatically be generated, based on your responses.

Market Analysis

Q.1 Describe the types of people you want to reach.

Q.2 What role do they play in the decision-making process?

Q.3 What factors stimulate and influence their buying patterns?

Identifying Competitors

In simple terms, your competitors can be identified as those companies that offer similar products or services to the same customers at similar prices. These can be either direct or indirect competitors.

As an example, Kodak identifies Fuji as a major or direct competitor for camera products. However, they also face competition from companies that offer different products, but ones that supply the same service or capability, i.e. indirect competitors which are companies like Nokia who offer mobile phones with digital cameras as an integrated feature.

Identifying who your competitors are and understanding the approach they take in the market can help you to develop and sustain a competitive advantage.

The following questions can assist you in identifying and understanding your competitors:

- » Can you make a list of your top five or ten direct competitors?
- » Can you identify any indirect competitors to your product or service?
- » Do you know what your competitors are doing, i.e. what are the benefits of their products and how are they marketed?
- » What are your competitors' strengths and weaknesses?
- » What do consumers think about your competitors' products?
- » How are you going to position yourself in comparison to your competitors? Would it be meeting the competition? Beating the competition? Countering the competition?
- » Are you competing on price, product, quality or another point of difference?

When analyzing competitors, it is important to identify their mix of objectives and the importance of each. For example, some competitors may be focused purely on profits while others may be focused on customer service.

Understanding the relative importance the competitor places on profitability, growth, market share, technology etc can assist you in understanding how your competitors may react in different competitive situations.

Build your Marketing plan

Build your business plan by answering the questions

below. A plan will automatically be generated based on your responses. Avoid changing your answers offline as they will not be saved to your profile.

Market Analysis

Q.1 Identify three of your major competitors.

Q.2 Identify the products/services that they offer.

Q.3 Describe the products/services that they offer.

Q.4 What factors contribute to their success?

Q.5 Assess their weaknesses.

Q.6 How will you address their strengths and capitalise on their weaknesses?

Q.7 What are their current market shares?

PEST Analysis

It is very important to consider the external environment that your business operates in before beginning the marketing process and just as important to continue monitoring for any changes that may influence your marketing activities.

To do this you can develop a PEST (Political, Economic, Social & Technological) model to help you identify and understand the various environmental factors that can impact your business and its marketing activities.

Political and Legal Factors

You are required to comply with laws and regulations designed to ensure markets operate with appropriate levels of competitive pressure to protect consumer rights and maintain market efficiencies. In Australia, the Competition and Consumer Act 2010 (CCA) aims to enhance the welfare of Australians through the promotion of competition and fair trading and provision for consumer protection.

It is important, when developing marketing initiatives, to be aware of any relevant restrictions under the Trade Practices

Act to avoid potential fines, negative publicity and expensive civil damage suits. There are also many laws and regulations in place with respect to advertising on the internet and dealing with disadvantaged or vulnerable consumers.

Economic Factors

Economic conditions can greatly affect levels of disposable income for consumers and influence the prices they are willing to pay, and the types of purchases they will make. For example, an economic recession or slowdown may reduce the consumers' disposable income, thereby reducing the consumer spending to the lowest level. At this stage, markets often lower prices and increase promotions to stimulate demand as much as possible.

Other factors that can affect the economic environment are inflation levels, unemployment, income and resource availability.

Social and Cultural Factors

A successful marketing strategy should reflect the needs and wants of consumers. For example, a greater emphasis has now been placed on environmentally-friendly products and services. As a result, Virgin Blue Airlines now offers customers the opportunity to offset their carbon emissions for each flight by paying a slightly higher fare during the booking process.

Technological Environment

It is important to monitor advances in technology and consider adopting new technologies that can increase your marketing capabilities. The internet is a technology that continuously improves and often provides to introduce new ways of doing things that often result in greater efficiency and effectiveness.

The internet offers excellent opportunities to cost-effectively research markets, analyse competitors and identify other ways to improve your business.

Build your Marketing plan

Build your business plan by answering the questions below. A plan will automatically be generated, based on your responses.

Market Analysis

Q.1 What are some of the political and legal factors that may affect your business?

Q.2 What are some of the economic factors that may affect your business?

Q.3 What are some of the social and cultural factors that may affect your business?

Q.4 What are some of the technological factors that may affect your business?

Marketing Research

Marketing research is the process of planning, collecting and analysing information that is related to a marketing decision that you have to make. Marketing research is vital as it provides you with the specific information you need to breakup or segment markets, decide on which areas to target, and to help identify the best way to position your business relative to your competitors.

As a fundamental part of business planning, market research can assist you by:

» Identifying new customers
» Understanding the size and nature of markets
» Improve understanding of current customers
» Setting of achievable goals and targets
» Formulating strategies
» Developing solutions to business problems
» Planning for business growth

» Identifying new opportunities.

While good research can assist you greatly, poor or inaccurate research can lead to bad marketing decisions, so it is critically important to plan and undertake your research as effectively as possible.

Steps involved in marketing research include:

Step 1: Identifying and defining your problem:

Prior to carrying out your research it is best to gain an understanding of what your objectives are.

For instance, your problem may be whether to introduce a new product or not so your marketing research would then be based on assessing the market to identify whether the market would accept this product.

Step 2: Designing and planning your research:

Designing and planning your research carefully helps to get you the best results and can save you time and money.

The two main sources of research include primary research, i.e. gathering information that does not already exist and is for your specific purposes and secondary research, that is gathering information that has been previously collected for any purpose other than your specific needs.

Primary research is usually conducted through interviews or surveys and while offering the best chance of obtaining highly relevant information for your specific purposes it can be expensive as it is time consuming and often requires outsourcing to a specialist provider.

Secondary research is often more cost-effective as it can be undertaken using any source of existing published information. Popular sources of secondary data include government websites, government department sites and industry associations.

It is best to start planning your research by evaluating

what data and information is in existence and then determine the specific areas where you may need to conduct primary research.

Collecting Data and Information: Some common techniques used to collect data and information include:

» Online surveys
» Telephone interviews/in- home personal interviews
» Questionaires

It is important to consider the type of data and information you require, to match the best possible collection techniques for each requirement.

Step 3: Analysing data and information

Once data and information have been collected, the next step is to organise the information and interpret it in accordance with your research objectives to draw a conclusion and define what choices you have available as the next steps.

The key to market research success is a systematic approach and the completion of each step before the next starts.

Step 4: Using market research

Once the outcomes of your research are available, you can feed the information into the formulation of your marketing strategy. However it is important to remember that if the outcomes of the research activities are not sufficient to make a decision, you may need to conduct further research as required.

Step 5: Preparing a report

It is good practice to always compile your research outcomes into a report with recommendations for further actions. Even if it is purely for your own use in the case of a micro business, preparing the information into a structured report helps to ensure your information is credible and justifiable.

If you are working in a larger organisation, it will be important to be able to effectively communicate the research outcomes to your colleagues.

Build your Marketing plan

Build your business plan by answering the questions below. A plan will automatically be generated, based on your responses.

Market Analysis

Q.1 What types of market research have you undertaken?

Q.2 How far back will your research go?

Understanding Market Trends

Identifying and understanding trends in the market assists you to forecast future sales and anticipate events and changes that can impact your business. Trends in the market can be identified by understanding the pattern of growth or decline in sales resulting from changes in environmental factors such as:

- » Seasonality
- » population
- » social
- » technology
- » economic cycles
- » political climate

Trend analysis can look at short, medium and long-term trends and can provide information on growth and decline rates for overall markets and individual segments.

Build your Marketing plan

Build your business plan by answering the questions

below. A plan will automatically be generated, based on your responses.

Market Analysis

Q.1 What trends have previously affected this industry?

Q.2 What current trends are affecting the industry?

Q.3 What trends may affect this industry in the future and how?

Q.4 Is this industry governed by legislation?

Q.5 What impact does it have on the industry and the success of your business?

SWOT Analysis

Once you have identified your customers, competitors and the trends in the market, the next step would be to have an understanding of where your product has been recently, where it is now, where it is headed in terms of your plans and the external factors and trends affecting it.

You can develop this understanding by carrying out a SWOT analysis.

A SWOT analysis is based on identifying your business' internal strengths and weaknesses and the external opportunities and threats.

It is important to remember that the goal is not simply to develop the SWOT analysis, but to transfer the result of the analysis into action in order to help your strategy grow and succeed.

Therefore, the final goal of the SWOT would be to identify the critical factors affecting your organisation and then build on your strengths to reduce your weaknesses, exploit opportunities and avoid the potential threats.

As illustrated through this example, carrying out a SWOT may enable you to identify various factors influencing your business:

Strengths
- » Cost Advantages
- » Financial Resources
- » Customer Loyalty
- » Wide recognition for social responsibility

Weaknesses
Need for experienced managers to help growth
Inadequate financing capabilities
Weak market image

Opportunities
Growing demand for quality
Enter new markets
Acquire firms with needed technology

Threats
Changing buyer tastes
Likely entry of new competitors
Adverse government policies

Build your Marketing plan

Build your business plan by answering the questions below. A plan will automatically be generated based on your responses.

Business Profile

Q.1 List some of the strengths of your business.

Q.2 List some of the weaknesses of your business.

Q.3 List some of the opportunities that exist for your business.

Q.4 List some of the threats that exist for your business.

Market Differentiation

Points of Difference

The positive ways in which your product differs from your competitors is referred to as differentiation. Points of difference are the individual characteristics of a product or service that establish differentiation.

Points of difference are usually in line with the unique selling and are critical in defining the competitive advantage of your products.

In order to gain a competitive advantage from points of difference, they must be benefits that your consumers strongly, uniquely and positively associate with your product, rather than any competing product.

Once you have clearly communicated the points of difference to your customers and your customers accept them, your brand will be set apart from your competitors.

Points of Parity

It is also important to make sure that your customers understand the specific product category to which your product belongs.

Points of Parity can be viewed as certain features that are shared by members within a certain product category.

The question to ask in this instance is whether you can at least match the competitors' claimed benefits.

For example, defining Subway as a fast food restaurant like McDonalds or Hungry Jacks would mean that Subway provides quick service, numerous products and low prices.

This would also help customers label Subway as a fast food restaurant.

Build your Marketing plan

Build your business plan by answering the questions

below. A plan will automatically be generated, based on your responses.

Product/Service Overview

Q.1 Identify and describe the points of difference between your product / service and those of your competitors.

Marketing Planning

This chapter assists you in understanding important concepts in marketing planning, such as market segmentation, targeting and positioning. It also views the marketing mix as a tactical strategy in marketing planning and thereby discusses the four main variables that are used to achieve your marketing objectives.

Business Description

A business description allows you to get your ideas, plans and visions down on paper before you go any further. It is important to have a thorough understanding of what your business is, and the direction that you intend it to follow.

To help you develop your business description, you can brainstorm all of your ideas about what your business will be and the products and services you will provide to consumers.

Some questions to consider when brainstorming include:

- » What is the main purpose of your business?
- » What products and services will your business provide?
- » Who will be your customers/suppliers?
- » What will your role be within the business?
- » Does your business have future growth potential?
- » How profitable could the business become?
- » What will the business be in five years time?

The business description does not need to be overly

extensive or detailed. It is mainly to provide an outline of what will be further explored in the business plan.

Build your Marketing plan

Build your business plan by answering the questions below. A plan will automatically be generated, based on your responses.

Business Profile

Q.1 What is your business' trading name?

Q.2 Are you starting a new business, buying an established business, starting a franchise, or are you an independent contractor?

Q.3 Describe the ownership of the business.

Q.4 Describe the products/services that your business will offer.

Q.5 Where will your business be located?

Q.6 Why is this location ideal?

Market Segmentation

Market segmentation involves grouping your various customers into segments that have common needs or will respond similarly to a marketing action. Understanding the concept of segmentation is central to marketing because each customer group will require a different marketing mix strategy.

Furthermore, each segment will offer differing growth and profit opportunities so the trick is to deliver the best offer to the best segment.

Some different ways you can segment your market include

the following:

- » Demographics: focuses on the characteristics of the customer. For example age, gender, income bracket, education, job and cultural background.
- » Psychographics: the customer group's lifestyle. For example, the social class they belong to, lifestyle, personality, opinions, and attitudes.
- » Behaviour: is based on customer behaviour. For example, online shoppers, shopping centre customers, brand preference and prior purchases.
- » Geographical location: such as continent, country, state, province, city or rural area the customer group resides.

Build your Marketing plan

Build your business plan by answering the questions below. A plan will automatically be generated, based on your responses.

Market Analysis

Q.1 Identify and describe the various market segments.

Targeting

Once you have segmented your market based on different characteristics, the next task is to choose one or more target market segments.

Developing different marketing strategies for different customer groups is very important as no one particular strategy would satisfy all customer groups with different characteristics, lifestyles, backgrounds and income levels.

There are three general strategies for selecting your target:

Undifferentiated targeting

This approach views the market as one big market with no

individual segments and therefore uses one single marketing strategy. This strategy may be useful for a business with little competition where you may not need to tailor strategies for different preferences.

An example of when undifferentiated targeting can succeed is if your business is the only one of its kind in a small isolated town where you would consider all people living in the town as your target market. However this strategy may not be effective if there are three or four competitors also in town.

Concentrated targeting

This approach focuses on selecting a particular market niche for targeting the marketing efforts. Because your firm is focusing on a single segment you can concentrate on understanding the needs and wants of that particular market intimately. Small firms often benefit from this strategy as focusing on one segment enables them to compete effectively against larger firms.

Porsche for example, targets an upscale automobile market through "Class appeal, rather than mass appeal".

Multi- segment targeting

This approach could be selected if you wish to focus on two or more, well defined market segments and want to develop different strategies for them. Multi-segment targeting offers many benefits to firms including greater sales volume, higher profits and large market share.

However, this method can be costly as it involves greater input from management, increased market research, and increased promotional strategies etc.

Prior to selecting a particular targeting strategy, you should perform a cost benefit analysis between all available strategies.

MARKETING AND SALES

Build your Marketing plan

Build your business plan by answering the questions below. A plan will automatically be generated based on your responses.

Market Analysis

Q.1 Will the target market be local, national, international, or a mix?

Q.2 Will your product/service meet the needs of the target market? If so, how?

Q.3 Describe your strategy for approaching the target market.

Positioning

Positioning is developing a product and brand image in the minds of customers or developing a perception in the customers' mind of the experience they will have from purchasing your product or service.

The business can positively influence the perceptions of its chosen customer base through strategic promotional activities and by carefully defining your business marketing mix.

Effective positioning involves a good understanding of the positions occupied by competing products and the benefits sought by the target market. It also requires identifying the differential advantage with which it will deliver the required benefits to the market against the competition.

Businesses which fail to implement effective positioning can fail to establish a clear perception of their business in customer's minds and hence lose ground in the market to competitors that have a clear position.

For example, Ferrari is positioned in the prestige segment of the car market with a differential advantage based on high performance and exclusivity.

Some other car industry examples of strong positioning include:

Volvo - safety, quality medium to high price
Mercedes - luxury and high price
Holden - quality family cars medium price
Hyundai - low price

Build your Marketing plan

Build your business plan by answering the questions below. A plan will automatically be generated, based on your responses.

Market Analysis

Q.1 What is the positioning strategy for your product/service?

Marketing Mix

Once you have decided on your overall competitive marketing strategy, you can then focus on planning the details of your marketing mix. A marketing mix is a set of controlled variables that formulate the strategic position of a product or service in the marketplace.

The primary goal of marketing is to optimise the marketing mix, offering the best possible combination of the four P's to maximise the effectiveness of marketing efforts.

The variables known as the four P's of the marketing mix are:

1) Product
2) Price
3) Place
4) Promotion

Product

Product is the mix of all the features, advantages, and

benefits that you offer to your target market. It may include certain characteristics such as quality, packaging, after-sales support, customer services etc. In order to ensure that your customers are gaining the full benefits of your product, you can consider the following questions.

- » What is the core benefit your product offers? For instance, customers who purchase mobile phones buy more than just a phone; they purchase the ability to keep in touch.
- » What does the actual product include? This includes branding, additional features and benefits that provide differentiation and ensures that customers will purchase your product over the competitors.
- » What non-tangible benefits can you offer? Factors to consider at this point may include after-sales service, warranties, delivery etc.

Price

Price relates to the pricing strategy of your products or services. It may include discounts, trade-in allowances and credit terms to adjust for the competitive situation in order to bring the price into line with the buyer's perception of the value of the product. Businesses may use different pricing strategies, based on different situations.

These are listed below:

- » *Premium Pricing* - is used where a business may feel that there is a substantial competitive advantage for its products. Such high prices may be charged for luxurious products such as rare automobiles, first-class airline services etc.
- » *Penetration pricing* - may be used where a business would set a price lower than the general market price in order to increase sales and market share. Once this is achieved, the prices would be increased.

Penetration pricing would normally be most suitable for products with high price sensitivity whereby a small change in price would result in a large change in demand.

» *Skimming Pricing* - involves setting a high initial price relative to the prices of competing products. Price Skimming works best for prestigious products since buyers tend to be more prestige-conscious rather than price-conscious. Due to the initial high prices, the skimming strategy may also enable the organisation to recover its product development costs at an early stage. Once the product has been in the market for a short period, most businesses tend to lower prices over time, making the product available to a wider market.

» *Competition Pricing* - involves setting prices in comparison with your competitors. This pricing strategy is one of the most common strategies used by small retail businesses as an attempt to avoid price wars and still maintain a stable level of profit.

Place

Place refers to where the sales are to be made and how the products will be distributed. It includes: channels of distribution, the extent of market coverage, managing inventories, transportation and logistics. Put simply, Place involves all activities that deliver the product to your target customers.

Organisations that facilitate the movement of products from the manufacturer to the final user of the product are known as intermediaries. The common types of intermediaries include:

» Retailers: Those companies that sell mainly to consumers and determine the final selling price of the product.

» Wholesalers: Those companies that purchase merchandise in bulk from producers and resell mainly to businesses, the government and other retailers.
» Agents and brokers: Those firms do not take the title or ownership of goods and services but facilitate the sale of products from the manufacturer to the end user and take a commission upon the sale of goods.

With the rapid advancement of internet technology and increasing broadband uptake there is currently a move towards selling goods online particularly with the increased use of e-commerce technology.

As the internet facilitates a geographically dispersed market, firms are now able to reach a wider audience with a low setup cost.

Promotion

Promotion refers to the promotional activities that communicate the merits of your product to your target market in an attempt to persuade them to purchase it.

It may include various methods of promotions such as direct marketing, advertising, personal selling, sales promotions etc.

Build your Marketing plan

Build your business plan by answering the questions below. A plan will automatically be generated based on your responses.

Product/Service Overview

Q.1 Describe your products/services.

Strategy

Q.2 Describe your products/services.

Q.3 What makes your product/service unique?

Q.4 Describe the demand for your product.

Q.5 Describe your pricing strategy and how it lines up with your market.

Q.6 Why do you think this strategy will be effective?

Q.7 How competitive is your product/service price compared with your direct competitors?

Q.8 How will you get the product/service to the end-user and what channel of distribution will you use?

Q.9 What systems will be implemented for processing orders, shipping and billing?

Advertising & Promotions

This chapter assists you in understanding the advertising and promotional tools that are used in marketing products and services. These tools include advertising, direct mail, personal selling, sales promotions, public relations/publicity, and online marketing. It also discusses the long-term benefits of integrated online and offline offerings.

Advertising

Advertising is an important consideration for your business. It lets your customers know what your business is and the products/services offered, as well as encouraging them to buy from you, rather than your competitors.

As most small businesses cannot afford expensive advertising campaigns, it is very important to assess the different methods of advertising and select which methods will be most effective in reaching your customers.

Prior to advertising, ask yourself the following questions:

- » Is it going to put me in front of my target market?
- » What will it cost and what are the cheaper ways to reach customers?
- » Will this harm my image?

- » Is it likely to generate sales or if not, increase my profile?
- » Is it promoting features and benefits that are relevant to my target customers?

Following are some low-cost advertising options that are often a good solution for small business:

- » Print copy and online.
- » Local and online directories.
- » Use signage on your vehicles, stationery and any shop fronts.
- » Exchange fliers with other non-competitive businesses who could display them at their location. Also find locations such as shopping centres where you could post a flier on a bulletin board.
- » Consider advertising on the reverse side of receipts with major supermarkets such as Woolworths or Coles. This will help you get noticed by potential customers as people tend to go grocery shopping regularly.
- » Hand out your business card to as many people as possible and network regularly to make new contacts.
- » Advertising on the radio and sending out catalogues may be useful when you have large-scale sales.
- » Traffic pulling displays (trailers with billboards towed behind cars or trucks) during holiday seasons may also be an effective promotion tool.
- » Provide free t-shirts and other giveaway items with your logo to your staff and customers to wear.
- » Advertising on the sides of buses.

One of the main benefits of advertising for your business is the ability to communicate to a large number of people at one time.

Build your Marketing plan

Build your business plan by answering the questions below. A plan will automatically be generated, based on your responses.

Strategy

Q.1 What is your advertising strategy, how does it support the desired positioning of your business?

Q.2 How does your advertising and promotion strategy reinforce the customer benefits available through your unique selling proposition (USP)?

Q.3 How does your advertising and promotion strategy focus your promotion efforts and spend on your identified target market?

Q.4 List and describe the forms of advertising you will use to promote your product/service and the frequency of the advert?

Q.5 What is the total cost of all your advertising efforts?

Direct Mail

Direct mail advertising is one of the most common promotional methods in direct marketing.

Direct mail advertising involves various printed material that can be sent to consumers in order to inform them about different offers or promotions. Common forms of direct mail advertising includes letters, newsletters, brochures, fliers, inserts into newspapers or magazines and emails.

Timing is an important consideration in direct mail advertising. For example, direct mail advertising carried out in December may not be as effective as customers are likely to disregard it due to the heavy mail flow during the Christmas period.

However direct mail advertising would be more preferable

during less competitive periods where you would have a better chance of standing out.

Apart from the timing of advertising, direct mail advertising often requires a strong follow up to be successful.

Build your Marketing plan

Build your business plan by answering the questions below. A plan will automatically be generated based on your responses.

Strategy

Q.1 List and describe the forms of direct mail you will use to promote your product/service. Will this be seasonal?

Q.2 Why are these forms of direct mail the most effective and how will they benefit your business?

Personal Selling

Unlike advertising, personal selling is a face-to-face sales activity that occurs between the buyer and the seller.

The main objective of this type of activity is to focus on developing a relationship with the potential buyer, with the aim of converting customer interest into a sale. This may be a short-term relationship involving only a single or few transactions as could be the case in a retail setting, or a long-term relationship involving multiple interactions and repeat business as may be the case in a business to business scenario.

Personal Selling provides the valuable opportunity to directly communicate with new and existing customers, allowing you to gain a personal insight into customer preferences and their feelings about your offering, allowing you to feed this information into your marketing mix.

In the situation where you have multiple sales people, it is essential that they are all 'on the same page' in terms of understanding the product/service thoroughly and presenting the correct image and information to your customers.

Build your Marketing plan

Build your business plan by answering the questions below. A plan will automatically be generated, based on your responses.

Strategy

Q.1 What sales method will you use (brokers, commissioned salespersons, etc)?

Q.2 Why is this the most effective selling process, how will it benefit your business?

Q.3 What tools will be provided to salespersons to assist in achieving sales?

Q.4 Will you be offering incentives to salespersons for achieving set goals? If so, describe.

Q.5 What training will be provided to assist staff in achieving sales objectives?

Q.6 What is the total cost of training your sales staff?

Sales Promotions

Sales promotions are activities that are usually short-term, designed to quickly stimulate demand by encouraging customers to purchase your products or services.

These may include coupons, free samples, contests with attractive prizes, organising demonstrations and exhibitions, interest free periods and temporary price reductions.

For retailers, sales promotions can be seen as an effective way for you to increase store traffic as various incentives may motivate consumers who are not store-loyal to visit your store. However sales promotions generally should not be the sole basis for your promotional campaigns as it is only a short-term promotional technique, and sales will often decline sharply once a special deal ends.

Advertising support is often needed in order to convert the customers who tried the product during the sales promotions into a long-term buyer. You should also remember that sales promotions should not be a continuous process. If sales promotions are conducted regularly they may lose effectiveness and customers may delay purchasing a product until another special deal is offered.

The following factors should be considered to increase the success of your sales promotions:

- » Develop a promotional plan or action plan that determines the promotion objectives, budget and suitable time span etc.
- » Design a creative message that focus on the unique selling proposition and clearly promotes the customer benefits of the offer.
- » Always try to be conscious of any similar competitor offers and try and differentiate your promotion where possible.
- » Ensure you maintain credibility by only offering what you can actually deliver, you don't want to fall short of the promise to customers and create customer dissatisfaction
- » And create customer dissatisfaction
- » Be open about any conditions that apply to an offer and do not try to hide them. You still need to comply with all obligations under any other applicable laws or regulations when running a sales promotion.

Build your Marketing plan

Build your business plan by answering the questions below. A plan will automatically be generated based on your responses.

Strategy

Q.1 List and describe the forms of sales promotions you will use to help sell your product/service. Will this be seasonal?

Q.2 Why are these forms of sales promotions the most effective and how will they benefit your business?

Q.3 What is the total cost of all your sales promotional efforts?

Public Relations

Public relations, often referred to as PR, involves managing communication between your organisation and any individual or group that is connected to, or affected by it in some way.

This could be your customers, suppliers, employees, government or the general public. Public relations can have various goals including education, building or improving a brand or image.

PR can get an organisation exposure to their audiences by using topics of interest and news stories that do not require payment. As PR provides exposure through credible third-party outlets, it provides more legitimacy than advertising as it is more independent.

Examples of PR include speaking at events such as conferences and fund raisers, sponsoring local sporting teams or community groups, working with the media by releasing news articles of interest, and communicating with employees and customers.

However, just as good PR can positively affect your business, any bad PR your organisation receives can be damaging for your reputation and overall business.

Build your Marketing plan

Build your business plan by answering the questions below. A plan will automatically be generated based on your

responses.

Strategy

Q.1 What is your strategy for achieving a positive image through public relations (PR)?

Q.2 Why is this the most effective method and what are the benefits for your business?

Q.3 Will you use external public relations agencies?

Q.4 How will you minimise potential negative PR?

Q.5 What is the total cost of all your PR activities?

Internet Marketing

The internet can be a great way to do business especially with the increase in the number of people with access to online facilities.

Online advertising is similar to print advertising in that it offers a visual message; however, it has some additional advantages in comparison to other modes of advertising.

Some of the advantages of internet advertising are:

- » Rich multi-media advertisements can be developed consisting of drop down menus, built- in games or search engines to engage viewers
- » Online advertising can be interactive, i.e. two way communication allowing the user to provide feedback and login registering their details
- » Online advertisement can be tailored or personalised for individual audiences, hence targeting different market segments
- » It offers an opportunity to reach younger consumers who have developed a preference for online communication

» Results from online advertising are measurable providing the opportunity accurately gauge the effectiveness of advertising campaigns

The most common forms of online advertising options include:

Banner ads

This form of advertising involves embedding an advertisement to a web page. Its main objective is usually to attract traffic to a website by linking via a click through to the website of the advertiser.

Search engine marketing

This form of advertising aims at promoting websites by increasing their visibility in search engine results pages. Most internet traffic begins at search engines like Google and Yahoo, you can increase search engine rankings by developing links to other sites within your site and adding fresh content related to keywords that are related to your products or business.

It is often useful to engage a professional search engine optimization (SEO) expert to assist you in improving your search engine ranking results.

Pay for placement

Major search engines now offer a facility called "Pay for Placement" also known as "Pay-Per-Click". When using Pay for Placement, advertisers bid on keywords or keyword phrases on which when searched by customers, their ads would be displayed.

Most advertisers would benefit from this option, as consumers would be attracted towards a particular product for which they otherwise would not have known.

Build your Marketing plan

Build your business plan by answering the questions

below. A plan will automatically be generated based on your responses.

Strategy

Q.1 Will you have a website for your business? If so will you have just simple promotion on the site or offer other features such as online catalogues or online ordering?

Q.2 Who will be responsible for developing, maintaining and ensuring that the website is being utilised effectively? E.g. search engines optimisation and affiliate exchange programs.

Q.3 What is the total planned cost of your online marketing efforts?

Online & Offline Integration

If you intend on carrying out both online and offline marketing for your business, an important point to remember is that isolating your marketing strategy as online and offline can cost you a lot in the long run.

Online marketing can benefit immensely from traditional offline marketing such as direct mail and advertising just as much as how offline marketing can benefit from promoting the business through the internet.

Therefore, as a small business with a limited budget, using both online and offline marketing together may help you get a better return on investment.

You may have an effective strategy for marketing over the internet, with a well established website with all the relevant information. However, you may wonder why your sales are not increasing and your return on investment is not what you expected.

At this stage, you may want to analyse how many people really know about your website and how many people were actually directed to your website.

The goal is to have all you marketing strategies supporting

one another.

For instance, you could use your URL (web address) on every letter, email or magazine that you publish as well as on your business cards.

Not only would this help increase the recognition of your business, this would also give your customers additional methods of accessing and purchasing your product.

Consistency

Integrating online and offline marketing efforts would also mean delivering information that is consistent with both modes of marketing.

For instance, if you use direct mail to communicate a certain sales promotion to your customers, you should make sure that the same message is communicated through the internet to the rest of the consumers.

If you fail to do this you may not be delivering the message accurately, which would result in disappointed customers.

Simultaneous marketing

You may also consider carrying out your online and offline campaigns simultaneously. This can be achieved by planning your campaign on a specific date and making sure everything is organised from both ends.

One way of succeeding this integration would be to distribute printed fliers about a certain promotion and directing customers to your website for more information.

Review & Improve

This chapter assists you in understanding the final steps of your marketing process which includes reviewing key performance indicators, monitoring performance and adjusting your marketing campaigns after careful review and evaluation.

What is an Action Plan?

An action plan integrates all of the strategies you have developed throughout your business plan into a highly organized and prioritised plan of action designed to achieve your stated business mission and goals.

This is achieved by breaking down the strategies you developed into small, achievable steps and then identifying the actions you need to take for each step. It can be used as a short-term (6-12 months) action plan to achieve short-term business goals, a medium term action plan (2-3 years) or a long-term action plan (3-5 years).

An action plan identifies the business goal (what you would like to achieve) and the strategies that can be implemented to reach that goal.

It also explains the specific actions that need to take place in order to achieve the business strategy. This will include the timeframe, roles and responsibilities, performance indicators and alternative methods that can be implemented to reach the business objectives.

Developing an Action Plan

Generally action plans are limited to a small and manageable number of goals. This helps to keep the plan realistic and achievable.

For each action you should identify:

» The timeframe and priorities for each action.
» The people who will be responsible for undertaking each action.
» Specific performance indicators to help you determine in the future whether your business has succeeded in achieving the business goal.

Once you have these details identified, you can progress to formulating a series of strategies to be undertaken to achieve the goals of each action item. It often helps to break the various strategies tasks down into simple and specific steps to keep the plan on track and avoid getting overwhelmed or losing control.

An important step is being able to evaluate within a set period of time if the action plan has been a success. Failing to do so could result in a plan that continues on indefinitely without ever actually achieving anything positive for the business.

To evaluate your action plan, go back to the initial objectives you set out and decide if they have worked, not worked or are in the process of being achieved.

Be critical of each objectives success or failure in this stage. If your original targets were too optimistic, then you need to admit this so that you will be able to move on.

Sometimes it may become apparent that an action plan has failed to meet its objectives. Therefore, you may need to reassess and redefine your original objectives and strategies to improve their success or abandon the plan and start again at the beginning rather than waste resources on a plan that isn't working.

Build your Marketing plan

Build your business plan by answering the questions below. A plan will automatically be generated based on your responses.

Implementation

Q.1 Develop an action plan that outlines the key tasks and activities required to implement your marketing plan.

Reviewing KPIs

An important final step of the marketing process is to review and make improvements to your plan.

To help you achieve this you can develop and monitor a set of measures to see how well your marketing strategy is working against the objectives you have set. These measures are commonly called Key Performance Indicators (KPI's).

When setting your objectives and KPI's, it is important to ensure they are practical. To help you do this you can use what is called the "SMART" test.

The Smart test ensures that your goals and KPI's are;

S - Specific
M - Measurable
A - Achievable
R - Realistic
T - Time bound

After your marketing strategy has been in place for a reasonable length of time, it is necessary to review its success and identify areas that need to be improved.

Over time, changes to your business can occur and you will need to reassess your marketing strategy accordingly.

The success of the marketing campaign can be measured by comparing its performance in the marketplace against what was originally laid out by the marketing goals. These goals are the key indicators for determining the level of performance your campaign has achieved.

If the marketing has met expectations and still fits within the SMART guidelines, you may not need to alter the objectives at all. However, if the objectives are not being met, you will need to either change the objectives to make them more realistic and achievable, or implement changes that will make the marketing more effective.

Build your Marketing plan

Build your business plan by answering the questions below. A plan will automatically be generated based on your

responses.

Implementation

Q.1 Have you developed a set of Key Performance Indicators (KPI's) to measure against your marketing objectives? Remember you can use the S-M-A-R-T approach.

Q.2 How often will you review your marketing strategy to ensure that it is still effectively working for your business?

Q.3 How will you assess the performance of your business in the marketplace?

Monitoring Performance

Regularly monitoring your marketing campaign is important for it to succeed. You will need to assess and analyse its performance to ensure that it remains effective. This will allow you to have better control over the performance of your marketing strategy.

One method you can implement to monitor the performance of your marketing plan is a marketing audit. A marketing audit is a comprehensive examination of your objectives and strategies to determine problem areas and opportunities for improvement.

A marketing audit uses a systematic approach to cover all areas of marketing in a business and does not simply focus on the problem areas. It is an independent review of the direction that your campaign has taken and its outcomes, compared to what was originally laid out by your marketing objectives.

They are generally performed by experienced people who are not directly involved in your marketing department.

In order to be a useful tool, a marketing audit should be conducted on a predetermined periodic basis. This is to provide regular updates and give you opportunities to improve the effectiveness of your marketing strategy.

You may also choose to conduct internal reviews and

monitoring of the performance of your marketing. These can be conducted as frequently as you need, or even run continuously to provide a regular summary of success.

By conducting analysis of your original goals, combined with the actual results of your marketing, you can set yourself benchmarks to improve upon.

You can implement strategies such as surveying customers to find out if the marketing campaign has had any influence on them as well as looking specifically at your sales records. You can then determine if there were new customers or more sales after the implementation of a new marketing scheme.

You can then gauge if the time and costs associated with the campaign have been effective, or if changes need to be made.

Build your Marketing plan

Build your business plan by answering the questions below. A plan will automatically be generated based on your responses.

Implementation

Q.1 How often will you conduct a marketing audit?

Q.2 Determine the costs associated with a marketing audit.

Q.3 How will success in meeting marketing objectives be monitored?

Q.4 How will the contribution made by promotional and advertising efforts be measured?

Q.5 Who will be responsible for conducting the audit? Will you be using the services of an independent auditing company?

Q.6 Will you be implementing any strategies to get feedback from your customers? E.g. customer feedbacks.

Adjusting a Marketing Campaign

After evaluation and review of your marketing strategies, you may be required to adjust your marketing campaign. This may be due to changes in the market or because the campaign is failing to meet its objectives.

Firstly this involves evaluation of performance against the original plan. If there is poor performance, you will be required to take corrective action to improve the situation. This may involve significant changes or changes at a strategic level or smaller tactical type changes.

Strategic control of your marketing campaign involves looking at whether or not your basic objectives still meet the possible opportunities. Often, marketing strategies can become outdated as the marketplace changes frequently. Your business should regularly reassess and modify your marketing programs accordingly.

Another important factor to consider when adjusting a marketing campaign is the costs and difficulties associated with making changes. You will need to assess all of the relevant and hidden costs of changing your campaign. A decision will then have to be made by comparing the possible benefits of making the changes with the costs involved.

If the campaign is significantly underperforming or it appears that the marketing strategy has failed, it may be necessary to return to the research and planning stage. You can either abandon the campaign altogether and write off the expenses as a mistake and then start fresh with a new campaign or you might seriously modify the objectives or strategy to try and improve performance.

Both have significant costs that need to be taken into account.

After implementing an adjusted or new marketing strategy, it is important to reassess and evaluate the changes after a short period of time. This will allow you to gauge if the changes are better, the same or worse when compared to the previous strategy.

Build your Marketing plan

Build your business plan by answering the questions below. A plan will automatically be generated based on your responses.

Implementation

Q.1 What procedures will you have in place to adjust your marketing campaign if it is necessary after a review?

NOTES

www.CEO-OnDemand.com.au
www.MoreProfitLessTime.com

3 MANAGEMENT

Understanding Leadership

This chapter will help you to develop your understanding of leadership; what leadership is and whether leaders are born or made. Various leadership theories and styles are also explained.

Owners and managers need to be lifelong students of leadership and continue to improve as leaders.

What is Leadership?

Leadership is a vital role in any organisation. It involves defining the direction of a team and communicating it to people, motivating, inspiring and empowering them to contribute to achieving organisational success. Leadership requires being strategically focused and applying behavioural techniques to build commitment and attain the best work from your people.

The ingredient of effective leadership are complex and are widely agreed to depend on the specific leadership situation, considering the difficulty of tasks, the degree of a leader's authority and the maturity and capabilities of subordinates. Leadership skills often take time to learn, because they are multi-faceted, behavioural and context dependent.

Becoming an effective leader is challenging to many new managers, but offers the rewards of successfully orientating peoples work to be most effective and achieving excellence in team performance. An understanding of the principles of strategic thinking, direction setting, communications and motivation provides a springboard for developing skills and an effective management style to suit your personality and leadership situations.

Successful leaders in business often demonstrate the following attributes;

- » Positivity, reliability and pro-activeness
- » Clear vision of business goals
- » A firm commitment towards meeting defined goals
- » An ability to effectively communicate their vision
- » Commitment to their team and to their organisation
- » Skilfulness in planning and developing strategies
- » A focus on motivation and setting clear directions
- » The adaptability to engage with the views and needs of team members
- » An ability to inspire employees to meet goals
- » Commitment to the happiness and wellbeing of their team
- » Honesty and openness with their team

Developing leadership capabilities requires you to understand your own strengths and weaknesses and to be willing to continuously improve your skills and knowledge as you gain experience.

By developing your understanding of leadership, you will be better equipped to inspire and motivate your team to achieve results for your organisation.

Are Leaders Born or Made?

In considering the extent to which leaders are born or made, there are many different views. It is commonly believed that certain people are natural leaders, particularly with reference to pivotal historical figures.

However, if this were entirely true, there would be little point in the rest of us attempting to learn about leadership. Many people find themselves in management roles where leadership capabilities are useful or even vital to success, and then learn and develop the necessary skills to be a leader.

A view consistent with modern theories is that leadership involves a combination of personality traits and many specific skills and capabilities learned over time and gained through experience.

An ability to effectively resolve complex situations is perhaps one of the most important traits of a leader. However, this doesn't mean that leaders are always the smartest person in the team or that they have the most technical knowledge.

Successful leadership allows the specific skills and knowledge of the leader and each of their team members to be brought together in the best way to allow effective directions to be set and good decisions to be made.

A person's character, personality and attitude may assist them to assume a leadership role. However, evidence suggests that very different styles of leadership are able to be successfully applied by leaders to suit their own personalities and different leadership situations.

While some people may feel more inclined and be better prepared to take on leadership roles, an understanding of leadership functions allows us to develop skills and capabilities to achieve a successful leadership style matching our own character and talents.

Some of the basics of good leadership can be self-taught, but many useful skills will be acquired through experience developed over time. You may be influenced by parents, teachers, employers or colleagues as well as by observing the behaviour and style of other successful leaders and seeking their advice.

By watching and analysing, you can develop your own leadership style based on what has proven effective for others. To build your leadership you can also seek feedback from your team and ensure that you learn from your mistakes.

As a leader, there is always more to learn in dealing with new situations and different personnel. Your observations, training, experiences and personality will all help to shape your evolving leadership style.

Some of the most important aspects of leadership are a strong commitment to setting effective and clear objectives and enthusiasm and commitment to developing your team's performance.

Leadership Theories

Trait theories and behavioural theories of leadership are two of the main historical theories developed in the quest to define what good leadership is.

The earliest of modern theories was the trait theory of leadership which sought to look beyond the idea of leaders simply as exceptional individuals by characterising the general qualities exhibited by successful leaders.

Trait theory

According to trait theory, specific traits and characteristics were believed to be associated with an individual's ability to lead. Lists of leadership traits may still be found in many texts, including physical and intellectual characteristics, personality traits, behaviours and skills.

While the existence of a clear relationship between leadership success and these traits has been disputed, developments of trait theory persists in later writing, such as recent research establishing a link between leadership and traits such as logical thinking, persistence, empowerment and self control.

Problems identified with traditional trait theory include evidence that different sets of traits will be more effective in different situations; that the long list of traits mixes very different qualities, such as skills, behaviours and abilities; and that traits may be culture and gender specific.

Behavioural Theory

Behavioural theories take a different approach, focusing more on patterns of leadership behaviour than on the individual leader.

It suggests that certain behavioural patterns may be identified as leadership styles. Applications of behavioural theory promote the value of leadership styles with an emphasis on concern for people and participative decision making, encouraging collaboration and team development by supporting individual needs and aligning individual and group objectives.

In practice, trait and behavioural theories may be used to develop our own ideas about successful leadership, and it may be useful to consider which leadership traits would be beneficial in particular situations.

It may also be instructive to consider how our behavioural style as a manager affects our relationship with the team and promotes their commitment and contribution to the organisational goals.

Situational theory

Situational leadership theories propose that the effectiveness of a particular style of leadership is dependent on the context in which it is being exercised. From situation to situation, different styles may be more appropriate.

An emphasis is placed on developing the ability to work in different ways and change management style to suit the situation.

Two common situational theories include Fiedler's contingency model and House's path-goal theory.

Fiedler's contingency model suggests that leadership effectiveness depends on both leadership style (being task or human orientation) and the degree to which the situation gives the leader control and influence.

Three factors affecting a leader's control and influence are identified:

- » - The relationship between the leader and followers, whereby support may more easily be gained by a liked and respected leader;
- » - The structure of the task, whereby clarity of the goals, methods and criteria will promote greater influence, and;
- » - The leader's positional power, which may afford the leader greater control.

While Fiedler's work specifically developed the idea of matching the work situation to suit a leader's style, contingency theories also help us to consider how leaders and their followers might behave in different situations.

Hersey and Blanchard developed an influential situational leadership theory that identified four leadership styles, which may be selected to suit different situations:

- » *Telling/Directing* - for unwilling or poorly resourced personnel
- » *Selling/Coaching* - for willing but less competent personnel

- » *Supporting/Participating* - for moderately mature personnel
- » *Delegating* - for highly competent and mature personnel

The path-goal theory proposes that the effectiveness of leadership is influenced by the interaction of leadership behaviour and contingency factors, including employee characteristics (ability, experience, need for achievement, etc.) and environmental factors (task structure, authority system, team dynamics, etc.).

Path-goal theory suggests that leaders should support their team by setting a clear path to follow and removing roadblocks in order to allow them to achieve their goals. The leader is expected to adopt different leadership behaviours fluidly, according to the situation.

Four leader behaviours are identified:

- » Directive path-goal clarification
- » Supportive leadership
- » Participative leadership
- » Achievement oriented leadership

In path-goal theory, the effectiveness of different styles of leadership style is dependent on the combination of a particular set of employee characteristics, task and environmental factors.

This suggests that an effective leader will utilise aspects from various leadership styles, depending on the individual situation.

Situational and contingency theories emphasise a need for applying different leadership styles to adapt to different situations and factors in the organisational environment and in the capabilities and degree of motivation of team personnel.

Leadership & Business

This chapter looks at the importance of leadership in business, the difference between leaders with managers, as well as common leadership qualities.

The delegation process, common leadership mistakes, and pointers about leading through a crisis are also outlined.

Importance of Leadership

In a competitive business environment, effective leadership is an essential requirement in order to achieve organizational goals. To do this, leaders must be able to provide inspiration, motivation and clear direction to their team.

For any type or size of business, effective leadership provides many benefits and will assist the organisation to achieve success and stability. In the absence of effective leadership, organisations often grow slowly and may lose their direction and competitiveness. Some of the ways in which leadership can benefit a business include:

» A clear vision: setting a clear vision and communicating it effectively provides employees with an understanding of the organisational direction and allows them to clearly understand their roles and responsibilities.

» Effective planning: a structured approach is able to generate a plan of action that will most effectively meet the organisational goals. An inclusive planning process also provides the opportunity for people to identify, contribute to, understand and achieve well defined objectives.

» Inspiration and motivation: the commitment and enthusiasm of a business leader shapes the common goals of the organisation and provides inspiration and motivation for people to perform at a high level.

- » New ideas: encouragement of people to openly contribute and discuss new ideas in a positive environment makes use of their diverse experience and ideas to improve a business.
- » Employee relations: an open and engaging relationship between a leader and their team members demonstrates that they are valued as an integral part of the organisation, creating a sense of ownership among team members and developing a closer alignment between individual and team objectives.
- » Crisis Management: Good business leadership can help a team remain focused during a time of crisis, reminding the team members of their achievements and encourage them to set short-term, achievable goals.

These are just some of the ways in which good leadership can have a positive impact on your business. Understanding these skills and applying the strategies will help you to become a better leader and could potentially make your business more successful.

Leadership vs Management

There are differences between leadership and management functions.

Leadership provides direction, encouragement and inspiration to motivate a team to achieve organisational success.

Management, by, is primarily an organisational role, co-ordinating people's efforts and the allocation of resources to maximize efficiency in achieving identified goals.

The distinction between leadership and management is quite useful in gaining a better understanding of these different functions in an organisation.

Leadership and management operate hand in hand. To be a good manager requires leadership skills, and an effective leader will be reliant on applying their own and others' management skills to achieve their vision.

The table below outlines some of the key differences between leadership and management:

Leadership Characteristics	Management Characteristics
Strategic and people oriented focus	Tactical and organisational focus
Setting of organisational direction and goals	Planning co-ordinated activities
Motivation and inspiration of people	Administering and maintaining systems
Establishment of principles	Formulation of policies
Building a team and development of talent	Allocation and support of human resources
Development of new opportunities	Solving logistical problems
Promoting innovation and invention	Ensuring conformance to standards and procedures
Empowering and mentoring people	Instructing and directing people
Risk engagement and instigation of change	Management and containment of risks
Long-term, high level perspective	Short-term, detailed perspective

Leadership and management are closely linked functions: each is complimentary to the other. Without efficient management, the direction set by a leader risks being unsustainable. Similarly, management exercised without effective leadership will perpetuate current activities and directions, without adaptation to meet strategic goals and without optimising team performance.

Leadership Qualities

Different leaders will display different leadership qualities, depending on the context and circumstances of a situation. A capable business leader will be able to use their leadership qualities to gain the trust, respect and commitment of their employees, and motivate them to achieve organisational goals.

Effective business leaders usually exhibit a combination of some of the following qualities:

- » Integrity: Good leaders often place great importance on ethical values. They choose to do "what is right", even if it is hard. In general, leaders with integrity are honest, truthful, fair, reliable and will not let their emotions affect their ability to do their job.
- » Self-Confidence: Strong leaders have a firm belief in their abilities. They generally remain confident at all times and demonstrate the ability to handle challenges and pressure.
- » Commitment: Successful leadership is impossible without firm commitment. Good leaders remain focused and dedicated towards their objectives and goals.
- » Enthusiasm: Effective leaders usually have a pro-active approach towards people, problems and possibilities. They are able to stimulate and evoke excitement amongst employees so that achieving organisational goals can be done in an energetic manner.
- » Self-awareness and adaptability: Skillful leaders exhibit an understanding of their own values, skills, strengths and weaknesses.

- They are often flexible and willing to continually improve their knowledge and skills to meet new challenges.
- Future vision: Successful business leadership involves creating a well founded vision of what can be achieved in the future and the best way to approach it.
- Creativity: Effective leaders are creative in their approach, developing new ideas to resolve current issues and implementing them effectively to prevent future recurrences.
- Ability to understand people: Good business leadership requires a clear understanding of human behaviour and the ability to develop open and honest relationships with their team to understand their abilities, concerns, interests and motivations.
- Ability to inspire and motivate: Successful business leaders may be charismatic, highly organised, and very motivational in their interaction with employees. They develop a culture of hard work and commitment, inspiring and motivating the team to perform at its best.
- Openness: Good business leaders are able to listen openly to the ideas, suggestions and opinions of their employees. They are willing to adopt new ways of doing things if they believe it will be beneficial for the organisation. They focus on creating a positive environment of mutual respect and trust that enables the business to be well prepared for new challenges.
- Communication Skills: Good communication skills are vital for effective leadership. Skillful business leaders are usually very clear, effective and influential in communicating their vision to employees. They continuously improve their communication skills and

learn new ways to remain effective in a constantly changing business environment.
- » Business understanding: Successful leaders will strive to have a clear understanding of their business, the environment in which they operate and their competitors. They will develop an awareness of the strengths, weaknesses, opportunities and threats for their business and focus on maximising resources to their full potential.
- » Decisiveness: This is the ability to exploit opportunities and make sound decisions, while minimising risk. Strong business leaders will usually conduct a risk and/or cost and benefit analysis prior to finalising any decisions that may potentially have major impacts on the business.
- » Ability to build effective teams: Effective business leaders have the ability to see the potential in an employee and successfully place them in a team where their skills and talent will be properly utilised. They also resolve disputes, encourage debate and fresh ideas and give the team direction towards achieving common goals.

Effective Delegation

An important aspect of leadership is the ability to effectively delegate tasks.

Delegation involves handing over the authority, responsibility, and accountability for performing specific duties to others, so that they may act on your behalf.

Leaders may have difficulty delegating tasks for several reasons.

For example, they may not have confidence that others will complete tasks satisfactorily; training people may appear to be excessively time consuming; and they may be concerned about losing control and authority. However, without delegation you may find that you become overloaded with work and may need to assign at least some responsibilities to others.

Effective delegation is beneficial for the organisation as a whole. It enables leaders to gain more time and flexibility to focus on strategic planning, in turn helping the business to improve overall work quality and achieve improved efficiency.

With a reduced workload, leaders can allocate their time and energy to tasks that are more important and crucial to the business. Employees will also have more room to grow and develop new skills as delegation extends their scope of responsibility and provides opportunities to take on new tasks.

Effective delegation starts with identifying tasks that are suitable to be delegated. For example, a leader may adopt the SMART approach while delegating, identifying tasks for delegation that are Specific, Measurable, Appropriate, Reachable, and Time bound.

Selection of a suitable candidate to assign to the delegated task is important to ensure a successful outcome. You need to be confident that your employee's interest, skills, knowledge and experience are appropriate for the selected task. It is better to start off by assigning simpler or less important tasks to people at first, then gauging their performance and making decisions for further delegation.

When delegating selected tasks to suitable employees, it is important to explain to them the importance, limitations, and the desired outcome of the assigned tasks. Encourage them to ask questions and clarify their responsibilities to avoid miscommunication and errors.

It is also vital to ensure that all the necessary information, training, and the authority to perform the task are available to delegates and that they are aware of their accountability.

Once delegates start performing assigned tasks, it is

beneficial to establish mentoring and feedback procedures to follow their progress. Regularly arrange open discussion sessions with them to review their performance, discuss areas of difficulty and encourage them to find solutions.

Seek opportunities to acknowledge their progress with a word of appreciation or a motivation reward wherever it aligns with the desired result.

Effective delegation is an ongoing process that not only enables your organization to accomplish business efficiency through increased participation but also helps your employees attain professional growth and success.

Motivating Employees

This chapter explains a number of popular theories of leadership, including the hierarchy of needs theory, motivator hygiene theory and equity theory.

Some motivational techniques such as effective job design, setting goals and providing feedback are also discussed.

Theories of Motivation

Motivation is what stimulates and drives an individual's intensity and commitment towards achieving a result. Motivation is made up of factors that are responsible for the increase in a person's normal level of input or application, with the knowledge that they will receive some form of reward.

There are many theories that have been developed to explain motivation, each taking a different approach and contributing new concepts. An understanding of these theories may help you to better understand your role as a leader and the importance of motivating your employees.

Some of the most influential theories of motivation are briefly outlined below:

Maslow's hierarchy of needs theory

This early but very influential theory separated a human's

basic needs into five distinct categories. These categories, placed in order from most fundamental to higher order as shown in the following diagram are; physiological, safety, love/belonging, esteem and self actualisation.

If physiological needs are not being met, there will be a noticeable physical effect on a person. A lack in meeting needs related to safety, love/belonging or esteem will give no physical indication, but can leave a person feeling anxious or tense.

The highest order motive is self-actualisation.

This refers to the motivation of an individual to reach their maximum potential, their desire for self-fulfilment or the opportunity to "to become everything that one is capable of becoming".

The hierarchy of needs suggests that satisfaction of low order needs precedes the satisfaction of higher order needs. Issues of esteem and self-actualisation may be of little interest to a person faced with insufficient security or physiological stress.

The need for self-actualisation becomes important and able to be satisfied when lower level needs have been met.

Herzberg's motivator - hygiene theory

Herzberg's Motivator – hygiene theory proposed a dual model of employee motivation factors. It describes two distinct categories: a specific set of motivating factors that contribute to job satisfaction and another set of environmental (hygiene) factors that contribute to job dissatisfaction.

Job satisfaction and job dissatisfaction are not opposites but co-existent perceptions affected by these different sets of factors.

The factors in the positive motivating category lead to job satisfaction. They are based around activities an employee does, such as completing challenging work and receiving recognition, gaining responsibility, promotion and achieving goals.

Environmental factors don't have the same positive impact on job satisfaction, but have an influence on job dissatisfaction. These factors include company policy, supervision, workplace conditions and salary. The theory suggests that these factors won't motivate an employee or make them satisfied with their job, but their absence will create job dissatisfaction.

Therefore, to effectively motivate staff, it is necessary to equally consider both motivating and environmental factors.

Addressing factors in the work environment will contribute to ensuring that employees are not dissatisfied, but the development of positive motivational factors leading to job enrichment is necessary to achieve high levels of performance.

Adam's equity theory

Adam's equity theory suggests that beyond the satisfaction of their needs, people seek fair treatment in the workplace in terms of the ratio of their efforts and their rewards, and compare themselves to those around them to assess whether they are being fairly valued.

An employee will feel undervalued if they believe they are contributing more than comparable employees and not being rewarded equivalently.

Their level of motivation will depend on perceiving to be fairly or advantageously treated, which they will evaluate in this comparative manner.

Demotivation from perceived unfairness may be manifested by different individuals in very different ways, ranging from a silent reduction in effort to disruption and hostility.

For the leader, this theory emphasises that an individual's motivational influences are not isolated. High levels of dissatisfaction and demotivation may occur where people perceive that they are being comparatively undervalued.

Motivational changes may occur even where a person's situation is not varied, but as a reaction to awareness of changes made for other staff or in other parts of an organisation.

The evolving theories of employee motivation suggest that there are many variables influencing how a person perceives their job and becomes motivated to achieve a high level of performance.

Enduring concepts - such as the hierarchy of needs, the different motivational effects of job enrichment and environmental factors, and the influence of people's perception of fairness - all provide tools to help analyse motivational influences and develop strategies to improve levels of motivation in a specific work environment.

Motivating through Job Design

An employer may incorrectly assume that money is the sole motivator for their employees. For many people, job design is as important as fair remuneration in motivating employees to be more effective.

Job design has an influence on employee motivation, job satisfaction and commitment to their organisation, all of which have a significant impact on the efficiency of your business.

Jobs are often designed in a way that encourages specialisation. Work is divided into specific tasks, with the employee assigned to each task becoming very skilled, accurate and efficient at performing it.

However, an often overlooked problem with specialisation is that it generally has a negative impact on employee motivation.

Whilst an employee may become very efficient and skilled at completing a repetitive task, the lack of variety in their day can lead to boredom and a feeling of detachment from the overall goals and success of the business. They feel that as long as they complete their job satisfactorily, there is no need to be concerned with any other aspect of the business.

A possible solution to this problem involves providing employees with more variety in their work. One technique to do this is introducing job rotation, where employees move between different jobs periodically.

Not only will this reduce the monotony of their work, but it will develop a team with a wider range of skills.

Another way to improve employee motivation is through job enlargement. This is where employees are gradually provided with more challenging work and greater responsibility.

Whilst you may think this would have the opposite effect, many employees enjoy learning new things and will get more fulfilment from their work if they are given extra responsibility.

This also helps you to increase the skill level of your team.

Job enrichment is another motivational technique that you may want to consider. It involves providing employees with more control over the work they do.

By providing them with more authority and responsibility, it may encourage them to seek out better and more efficient ways to accomplish their task, leading to a potential increase in productivity.

The more interesting a person's job is, the more likely they will be motivated to apply effort and maximise their productivity. The Job Characteristics Model helps to explain the benefits of job design.

Core Job Characteristics:

- » Skill Variety
- » Task Identity
- » Task significance
- » Autonomy

- » Feedback

Outcomes:

- » Motivation
- » Performance
- » Satisfaction
- » Reduced Absenteeism
- » Turnover

Psychological States:

- » Meaningful
- » Responsibility
- » Knowledge of results

The core job characteristics will enhance employees' job satisfaction and motivation, potentially leading to better outcomes for your business.

Well designed jobs that don't invoke boredom and which increase the job satisfaction of your employees may help you to improve efficiency, productivity and morale within your business.

In turn, this could lead to less staff turnover, absenteeism and potentially make your business more profitable.

How to Set Goals

The process of setting goals allows the vision of an organisation to be translated into actions and results. It is able to provide people with a clear statement of their direction, their tasks and performance measures, and to align the objectives and activities of a team to a common and co-ordinated path.

To avoid goals being in effect little more than ideas or a wish list, and potentially either not being achieved or not delivering beneficial results, the process of setting goals should be undertaken in a planned and committed manner and in coordination with both higher levels of strategic planning and day to day task management.

Setting of goals becomes most effective within a process of goal management that adopts a number of basic strategies to ensure that goals are well conceived, clearly defined, attainable and finally become achieved.

The starting point for goal setting is the vision for an organisation, department or team's future. This vision may represent what the organisation would ideally be like at some point in the future.

At an organisational level, the strategic vision may incorporate new products, business directions or growth projections and may have a relatively long time horizon, possibly 5 years, while a department or team's vision may be more specific in relation to their performance, capabilities or processes, and have a shorter time horizon.

It is clearly important that visions at different levels in an organisation are aligned.

Achievements that will allow the vision to be realised may be identified as the basis for organisational goals.

Prioritisation of goals is critical to allow sufficient focus and resources to be applied to the most important ones. Pareto's 80/20 principle which proposed that 80% of all effects will result from only 20% of all causes emphasises the importance of selecting and prioritising the goals to be set.

The participation of employees in setting goals is considered to be highly beneficial. This allows people to develop a better understanding of their team goals and why they are important. Through early participation, their commitment and motivation to achieve goals that they have contributed to and believe in will be stronger.

Goals should be specific and should be written down. This provides a clear statement of what is expected for everyone. It is important that goals are not set too high to be achievable, nor too low to be challenging and effective. Goals must be realistic.

The effective management of goals requires that they be broken down into specific and measurable objectives, activities and steps, and that it is made clear who is responsible for doing what. It is important that timeframes are set for each activity, fitting into an overall timeline for the main goal.

The allocation of necessary resources, tools and training and potential roadblock issues such as time competition from employees' day to day workloads should be carefully considered and addressed.

An activity considered essential to successfully achieving team goals is the monitoring of progress. A regular review process should be put in place to track progress and assess and revise activities according to their actual status.

The progress meeting provides an opportunity for achievements to be lauded, for difficulties to be raised and for additional activities to be scheduled. It promotes team communication and support, and may be used to maintain focus and motivation. As things progress, goals themselves may need to be revised to suit changing issues and conditions.

Setting and achieving goals is an important aspect of an organisation moving forward to successfully achieve its vision. A strong commitment to the process of developing and implementing goals, using established techniques, is needed to convert goals into reality.

Power & Politics

This chapter looks at the power of leadership and the impact that it has on the politics of an organisation. It addresses the ways in which leaders are able to influence those around them into working towards goals and analyse how leaders use their social power.

Influencing Others

As a business leader, the ability to influence people around you to support your goals is a valuable skill. Quite often the organisational authority you may have as a leader is not sufficient to ensure people will support your ideas and initiatives.

Beyond influencing your direct employees, it is also often necessary to gain support from colleagues and decision makers in the organisation over whom you have no authority.

Influence and power are closely interrelated aspects of leadership. As influence implies being able to affect other people's thinking or actions, the power of our influence is exercised through relationships.

This tells us that building strong and effective relationships throughout the workplace will enhance your influence. Your leadership qualities will also have an impact on your influence, with people more likely to support someone who has an engaging vision and who is credible and respected.

Three main styles of influence are generally identified; logical, emotional and cooperative.

A logical influencing style involves appealing to reason and intellect. People who influence others using this style will clearly and logically explain their reasons, drawing upon detailed, factual evidence and identifying the benefits that will be delivered to convince their audience that it makes sense.

An emotional influencing style tries to link goals or direction to an emotional motivator, such as making someone feel positive or included, or providing a sense of contributing in a valuable way. A positive emotional response will be more likely if the proposal aligns with their values and goals. Emotional influencing may utilise the positive and enthusiastic presentation of an appealing vision which people feel able to support.

Cooperative influence involves building relationships and

networks between a leader, people they are trying to influence and other stakeholders to gain their support. Willingness to support people's efforts and work on their behalf may be demonstrated by actions such as making resources available and addressing roadblock issues.

Encouraging and appreciating people's inputs and encouraging participation in defining actions generates alignment and builds their commitment to your goals. Strategically developing coalitions and alliances with other stakeholders and respected figures may be used to broaden your influence and support and leverage the influence of others. Developing cooperative support requires patience and commitment.

Another important aspect of influencing people is the principle of Reciprocity, which characterises influence as a form of exchange, whereby it is necessary to provide a benefit in some form to receive one back.

More specifically, the writer Cialdini has proposed that people feel a strong reciprocal obligation to return a favour that has been offered to them, hence suggesting that providing support to others, either employees, colleagues or leaders, may be well rewarded when you seek reciprocal support in return.

Effectively influencing people is a subtle skill developed through experience. Capable influencers will apply all of the above styles to suit different contexts and audiences. Opportunities to apply influence will be most effective if they are thoughtfully planned and carefully prepared for.

In today's business organisations where authority is less structured and workplace teams and relationships are increasingly fluid, the power of influence is an increasingly important leadership capability.

Social Power

The question of "What is Power" has been considered by many thinkers, and does not have a simple answer.

The power held by an individual may be drawn from many different sources, and how it operates is a complex aspect of human relationships. How power is exercised depends not only on those holding it but also on the legitimacy accorded to them by those being controlled.

Belief structures, culture and even our language affect perceptions of power and how individuals offer others power over them.

Within organisations, leadership and power are closely linked. The concept of social power refers to power exercised through the influence of the thoughts and actions of others, such as between a manager and their subordinates. A study of social power by French and Raven indentified five (later six) bases of power that fall into two categories.

Positional power sources include legitimate power, reward power and coercive power.

Legitimate power is given to a leader by an organisational structure or hierarchy. It is the power associated with a title or position that is afforded to a person while they hold that position.

Reward power and coercive power are also related to a leader's position, and depend on the extent to which they have authority to provide rewards and enforce punishments to obtain desired behaviours.

The effect of rewards may be highly variable, and even senior leaders may only have limited reward power. Coercive power is that of the gaoler, the sergeant or the boot-camp trainer. Its use is rarely appropriate in the work environment.

Business leadership requires more expansive and influential forms of power than that simply related to their position.

Several forms of personal power are identified by French and Raven.

Expert power stems from having skills, knowledge and understanding exceeding that of those around you. Demonstrated expertise lends others to seek your leadership in an area, and creates trust and respect in your opinions. Gaining a reputation for logical thinking allows your power base to be expanded in other areas.

Referent power is related to the concept of a leader's charisma. It is based on the power people will afford to someone because they are charming, likeable or respected. Celebrities wield considerable referent power, which is utilised widely for product promotion. Because of its influence, referent power may be considered as a responsibility.

Alone, it represents a potentially unstable power base but in combination with other forms of power it may be used to good effect.

Information power was later added to French and Ravens categories. It refers to the power derived from holding information that is critical to achieving organisational objectives.

Understanding the different forms of social power allows us to better understand the ways in which other people may be influencing us and how we may be able to develop our own expert and referent power to become more effective and positive leaders.

Organisational Politics

All organisations are subject to conflict and competition between the desires and interests of different departments, teams and individuals. Organisational politics refers to the processes through which these rival interests are played out and eventually reconciled.

While in an ideal organisation it may be hoped that decisions are made on a rational basis, politics is inherently non-rational and subject to power interactions between diverse interests.

Members of an organisation are at the same time cooperating to achieve a common goal and competing for rewards, and at times their personal interests may be at odds with the organisation's objectives.

It is through the political system of an organisation that rival interests are resolved. This system represents how power is applied and distributed in the organisation. Understanding the political system of an organisation is necessary for a leader to operate effectively and reach their goals.

A leader, exercising power, is able to have a strong influence on the political climate of an organisation through their decisions, their way of handling conflict and providing recognition, support and inspiration to their teams.

Negative organisational politics may be very destructive for an organisation. This has been identified as one of the major sources of stress within modern businesses. Negative politics includes the use of subversive methods to promote a personal agenda which may undermine organisational objectives, distract energy away from organisational goals and compromise the interests, cooperation and fulfilment of other employees.

Such tactics may include filtering or distortion of information, non-cooperation, allocating blame, reprisals, dishonesty, obstructionism and threats.

Impression management is another aspect of organisational politics that it is important to maintain an awareness of. The term refers to techniques of self-presentation where a person may purposefully control the information they put forward about themselves or their ideas to create a favourable impression.

For the leader this implies that everything may not always be as it appears. Studies have indicated that people using impression management may be more favourably rated by their supervisors than others.

On the other hand, being aware of the impression you are creating should be considered in building support for your own goals. The extent to which impression management is applied is an ethical question that relates to a leaders credibility and integrity.

Often, political behaviour and manoeuvring within an organisation is caused by uncertainty, such as unclear objectives, poorly defined decisions, competition and change. A leader's influence may be used to smother a political climate that promotes such negative politics.

By promoting a positive culture that values integrity, respect and fairness within their team, the leader is able to channel people's interests and energy away from negative political interplay and towards an alignment with organisation objectives.

Allowing team members to express their interests and demonstrating a commitment to support individual needs integrates their fulfilment into the work organisation and promotes the positive resolution of political conflicts.

Decision-making & Managing Conflict

This chapter looks at the importance of decision-making and managing conflict in your business. It discusses various approaches of decision-making and its impact on your team.

Also discussed are the different types of conflict that may arise in the workplace and how to best manage these.

Models of Decision-making

As a leader, you'll frequently be required to make decisions, which can have significant impacts on your organisation and team.

Therefore, you should have a good understanding of the different models of decision making and what's involved in making a good decision.

The first thing you should be aware of is the importance of critical thinking and its direct impact on effective decision-making. Critical thinking can be defined as raising what is subconscious in a person's reasoning to the level of conscious recognition.

Good leaders are usually critical thinkers as they understand the mechanics of reasoning and are able to use this to manage the unconscious influences that contribute and affect their decision-making process.

Generally, critical thinkers:

- » Continually question their own and other people's assumptions, reasons, motivations, and outlook
- » Do not focus on contradicting others when questioning but focus on their reasoning and perspective
- » Answer questions by asking more questions

Unfortunately, critical thinking does not come naturally to most people. Like everything else, it is a skill you must continually develop and refine. As a leader, critical thinking can prevent your subconscious emotions and reasoning from clouding your judgement and thus allow you to make better overall decisions.

There are two basic models used to describe the decision making process; the rational model and Simon's normative model.

The rational model proposes that people follow a rational, four step sequence when making decisions. The four steps are:

- » Identifying the problem

- » Generating solutions
- » Selecting a solution
- » Implementing and evaluating the solution

Some of the limitations not considered in this model are issues such as not having enough information relevant to the problem and also the fact that problems can change in a short period of time.

The normative model of decision making takes into account the fact that leaders are bound by certain constraints when making decisions. These constraints include personal and environmental factors that reduce rationality, such as time, complexity, uncertainty and resources.

The normative model suggests that decision-making is characterised by;

Limited information processing - there is a limit to how much information a person can manage.

Judgemental heuristics - shortcuts are used to simplify decision making.

Satisficing - choosing solutions that meet minimum requirements and are "good enough.

A leader will only be able to manage a certain amount of information at any one time, so they make judgements based on their previous experiences wherever possible to speed up the decision making process. Often choosing a solution that is "good enough", is considered effective when there are multiple solutions that will produce similar outcomes.

Most people use variations of these theoretical models to make decisions in their day to day lives. Developing your understanding of the decision making process can help you become a better and more effective leader.

Decision-making Styles

Generally people differ in their approach to making decisions, we can term this their decision making style.

One perspective of decision-making styles proposes that people differ along two dimensions in the way they approach decision making.

The first is an individual's way of thinking.

Some people tend to be rational and logical in the way they think or process information. A rational type looks at information in order and makes sure it's logical and consistent before making a decision.

Others tend to be creative and intuitive. Intuitive types do not have to process information in a certain order but are comfortable looking at it as a whole.

The other dimension describes an individual's tolerance for ambiguity. Again, some people have a low tolerance for ambiguity. These types must have consistency and order in the way they structure information so that ambiguity is minimised.

On the other hand, some people can tolerate high levels of ambiguity and are able to process many thoughts at the same time. When we diagram these two dimensions, four decision-making styles are evident: directive, analytic, conceptual and behavioural.

Directive Style:

A person has this style if they have a low tolerance for ambiguity and are efficient, rational, and logical in their way of thinking. They focus on the short-term and are quick to make decisions, usually resulting in a decision that has been made with minimal information and not carefully analysing other alternatives.

Analytic Style:
As opposed to the directive style, a person with an analytic decision-making style has greater tolerance to ambiguity. They are careful decision makers that like to be well informed and thoroughly assess their options. They usually have the ability to adapt or cope with unique and challenging situations.

Conceptual Style:
Conceptual decision makers are generally very broad in their approach and consider all available alternatives. They are long-term oriented and are usually capable of formulating creative solutions to problems.

Behavioural Style:
People with a behavioural decision-making style work well with others, are open to suggestions, and are concerned about the achievements of their team. They generally try to avoid conflict and place importance on their acceptance by others.

A good understanding of the various styles of decision-making each will allow you to recognise your own style and adapt accordingly to each situation.

Group Decision-making

There can be advantages and disadvantages in involving teams of people in decision making.

Some advantages include; accumulating more knowledge, taking a broader perspective and gaining support by letting individuals participate in the process.

Some of the disadvantages in group decision making include often a slower time to get a decision, a necessity for compromise which results in a less than optimal outcome and the potential for an individual or clique to dominate the group, negating its original benefit.

One difficult decision in itself for a manager or business

owner is determining when to engage a group, and the extent to engage a group to help make a decision or whether to go alone and make a decision individually.

As the advantages and disadvantages can be different for different situations, there are tools available to assist you in determining, if, when and how to make group decisions.

One such tool is the Vroom-Jago decision model.

The model begins by analysing individual situations with questions including;

- » As the leader, do you have enough information of your own to make a good decision?
- » Is the problem structured in that it is clearly defined, organised and has recognised solutions?
- » Do the members of the group have to accept this decision for it to work?
- » If you make this decision yourself, are you sure the group will accept it?
- » Are the group members aligned with the same goals that you are trying to achieve?
- » Is disagreement likely among group members in reaching a decision?
- » If it is determined that a group decision is the preferred option, some simple guidelines for the decision making process can help as follows;
- » Develop a clear understanding of the problem and the need for a decision
- » Develop a clear understanding of the requirements for an effective choice
- » Thoroughly and accurately assess all the positive qualities of alternative solutions
- » Thoroughly and accurately assess all the negative qualities of alternative solutions

Although group decision making can be effective, it can also have disadvantages such as;

- » Social pressure. The pressure to conform to the group can have adverse effects on the creativity of the individual group member.
- » Domination by a vocal few. Group members may be ignored and outspoken by members who speak the loudest and longest.
- » Goal displacement. The primary objective of making a sound decision may be affected by a member's personal considerations such as winning an argument, or getting back at another group member.
- » Groupthink. Groupthink occurs when group members try to minimise conflict and want to remain within the comfort zone of the group's consensus thinking. Creativity and independent thinking are usually the first things to be sacrificed, resulting in poor quality decisions.

Types of Conflict

In the workplace, conflict is inevitable, usually occurring when one party perceives that their interests are being opposed or negatively affected by another party. Conflict can produce either a positive or negative outcome.

By being able to identify potential conflict before it arises and knowing how to effectively manage it, you will be able to help your staff increase the chances of turning conflict into a positive outcome.

There are two types of conflict, functional and dysfunctional.

Functional conflicts

Functional conflicts are constructive, support your company's goals, and improve performance. It generally involves people who are genuinely interested in solving a problem and are willing to listen to one another.

Stimulating functional conflict is a great way to improve your team's performance and generate new ideas. It involves getting your team to either defend or criticise ideas, based on relevant facts rather than on the basis of personal preference or political interests.

There are two widely accepted techniques for doing this: devil's advocacy and the dialectic method.

Devil's advocacy

This method involves assigning a team member the role of a critic. This person should always question and critique any ideas that your team may have, usually resulting in critical thinking and reality testing. However, it is recommended that this role gets rotated amongst your team to avoid any particular person from developing a strictly negative reputation.

Dialectic method

This approach involves facilitating a structured debate of opposing views prior to making a decision. By hearing the pros and cons of all the different ideas, your team will have greater success in making sound decisions. However, it should be noted that a major drawback of this method is that the emphasis to win a debate often clouds the issue at hand.

Dysfunctional conflicts

Dysfunctional conflicts on the other hand, consist of disputes and disagreements that hinder your company's performance. This generally involves people who are unwilling to work together to solve a problem and is often personal.

When dysfunctional conflicts arise in the workplace, there are various methods for dealing with it, including: integrating, obliging, dominating, avoiding, and compromising.

Integrating

This method is also known as problem-solving and

generally involves encouraging opposing parties to confront an issue and cooperatively identify the problem, generate alternative solutions and select the most appropriate solution. Misunderstandings and similar disputes can often be resolved using this method.

Obliging

This occurs when a person neglects their own concern in order to satisfy the concern of the opposing party. A characteristic of this conflict management style includes playing down differences while emphasising on commonalities.

Dominating

Also referred to as forcing, people that adopt this approach often have an "I win, you lose" mentality. Dominating relies on formal authority to force compliance and is generally appropriate when unpopular but necessary solutions are implemented.

Avoiding

This involves either passive withdrawal from the problem or active suppression of the issue. It is generally appropriate for trivial issues or when the negative effects of confrontation outweigh the benefits of resolving the conflict.

Compromising

This is a give-and-take approach for resolving dysfunctional conflicts and is particularly useful when the parties involved possess equal power.

The following are some examples of situations that can produce either functional or dysfunctional conflict:

- » Incompatible personalities
- » Overlapping or unclear job boundaries
- » Competition for limited resources
- » Inadequate communication
- » Interdependent tasks

- » Unreasonable rules
- » Unreasonable deadlines or extreme time pressure
- » Collective decision-making (the greater the number of people participating in a decision, the greater the potential for conflict)
- » Decision-making by consensus
- » Unresolved or suppressed conflicts

As a leader or manager, you should be continually aware of staff interactions within the workplace. As such, you should carefully observe and react appropriately to these early warning signs as they have the potential to lead to major conflict, reduce morale, motivation and cause business inefficiency.

Managing Conflict

Conflict in the workplace can arise in many different forms, however, the three most common are personality conflicts, intergroup conflict, and cross-cultural conflict.

By understanding the causes of these conflicts, you will have a greater chance of successfully managing and reducing their negative impacts on your employees.

Personality conflicts

Personality conflicts can be defined as interpersonal opposition based on personal dislike and/or disagreement. It can arise from something trivial or major, such as an employee not liking another based on their dress sense, work ethic, attitude, or communication style etc.

As minor as it seems, if personality conflicts are not dealt with from the beginning, they can have serious effects on employee morale and significantly hinder team performance.

Therefore, as a leader or manager, it is crucial that you carefully select your team not only based on their ability, but also consider their compatibility and commitment to your company's work culture.

Another common cause of personality conflict is incivility.

Examples include the use of vulgar language in the workplace, or not cleaning up after using shared facilities. To combat this sort of behaviour, some organisations have resorted to workplace etiquette training for their employees.

However, as a leader or manager, you will have to lead by example and act as caring and courteous role models if that is what is expected from your employees.

Traditionally, personality conflicts were either ignored or a party to the conflict would lose their job. However, this may lead to discrimination lawsuits so there are more effective ways for dealing with personality conflicts.

The following are some suggestions for dealing with such conflict:

- » Investigate and document the conflict.
- » Attempt informal dispute resolution and encourage the parties involved to work out their differences in a constructive and positive manner.
- » Avoid dragging other team members into the conflict.
- » Do not take sides.
- » Seek help from human resource specialists or professional counsellors if you are still unable to resolve the issue.

Intergroup conflict

Intergroup conflict generally arises when there are conflicts of interests within competing groups within an organisation.

It is often the result of group cohesiveness, which is the "we feeling" that binds group members together.

Although a certain level of cohesiveness is essential for an effective team, too much can also generate adverse effects,

including:
- » Members of in-groups view themselves as a collection of unique individuals, while they stereotype members of other groups as being all alike.
- » In-group members perceive themselves in a positive manner and as politically correct, while other group members are negative and immoral.
- » In-groups view outsiders as threats.
- » Some other common causes of intergroup conflict include:
- » High levels of conflict within a group, often leading to conflict amongst other groups
- » Negative interactions between groups as a whole or individuals
- » Third parties engaging in negative gossip about a group

As intergroup conflict can seriously hinder your organisation's performance and productivity, there are certain things you can do to prevent or minimise intergroup conflict which include:
- » Providing team building exercises to reduce conflict within a group and prepare them for working with other groups
- » Encouraging friendships and good working relationships amongst different groups
- » Appropriately dealing with negative gossip as soon as they arise

Cross-cultural conflict

Cross-cultural conflict can be defined as conflict between individuals or groups that are separated by cultural boundaries.

In today's workplace, the ability to deal with people from

different cultures is absolutely critical in order to achieve success.

The main cause of cross-cultural conflict is miscommunication. For example, if you have employees from high-context cultures, such as Japan, China, Mexico and Arabic nations, you may find that they heavily rely on nonverbal communication to get their message across. In contrast, people from low-context cultures such as Australia, North America, Germany and Switzerland, usually prefer to use verbal and written communication to convey their message.

To avoid misinterpretation and misunderstanding with your employees, you should have a good understanding of key differences within different cultures. However, you should not stereotype a person based on their cultural background as you may often find that some people are able to easily adapt to their surroundings.

As cross-cultural conflict can have major impacts on the productivity of your team, you should always be proactive. Some of the ways to build cross-cultural relationships include:

- » Being a good listener
- » Being sensitive to the needs of others
- » Being cooperative, rather than overly competitive
- » Compromising rather than dominating
- » Regularly engaging in conversations to build relationships
- » Being compassionate and understanding

NOW…IMPLEMENT

You've just absorbed a lot of business-building insights that can help your business grow. But not if you choose to do nothing with this new knowledge.

I love hearing your success stories and the path to this success starts with small steps.

So… go on. Take them.

Here's to you building a better business and a very successful future.

John L Millar

AIMM - Dip Mgmt - Dip Hrm - Cert IV TAE - NLP Prac

Certified Business Advisor, Business Consultant, Professional Speaker & Elite Business Trainer

International Best Selling Author and Managing Director of:

www.ceo-ondemand.com.au

www.moreprofitlesstime.com

Finalist - 2014 Australian Institute of Management Business Excellence Awards

Nominee - 2015 Australian Institute of Management Business Excellence Awards

Nominee - 2015 Telstra Business Awards

Nominee - 2015 Small Business Awards

Nominee - 2015 IPPY Award

Finalist - 2015 Axiom Business Book Award

Nominee - 2015 Australian Small Business Champion Award

NOTES

www.CEO-OnDemand.com.au
www.MoreProfitLessTime.com

ABOUT THE AUTHOR

John Millar is the Managing Director, Senior Business Coach Trainer and Consultant with More Profit Less Time Pty Ltd and CEO-ONDEMAND. Along with his many other business interests, John is proud to have been an associate of the most successful coaching team in the world.

He is recognized as a global leader and has been benchmarked against over 1,300 colleagues in 31 countries. John has over 25 years of hands-on ownership, management, coaching, and entrepreneurial experience in a broad range of industry sectors, including retail, wholesale, import, export, IT, trades and trade services, automotive, primary production, food services, transport, manufacturing, mining, professional services, the fitness industry, and more.

He has extensive experience developing and providing training for small to medium-sized companies and a variety of publicly listed corporate companies. John is an accomplished and talented public and professional speaker. He has been a mentor working with sales/management activities for businesses with a turnover under $100,000 per annum, over

$100 million turnover, and everything in between, with great success.

John currently works with business owners and their teams across Australia and has a "Whatever it takes" attitude that has enabled him to help his clients grow their business profits by up to 800%.

If you are ready to be coached by one of the best in the business, register at:

www.ceo-ondemand.com.au

Make sure to visit www.moreprofitlesstime.com for the new online Management Development Program: *The Business Essentials Series.*

NOTES

www.CEO-OnDemand.com.au
www.MoreProfitLessTime.com

NOTES

www.CEO-OnDemand.com.au
www.MoreProfitLessTime.com

DISCLAIMER

The material available in this book, video file, audio file or any other medium is distributed as a general reference source. While every effort is made to ensure that the information is accurate, users must be aware that some information may not be accurate or is no longer current. The author makes this material available on the understanding that users exercise their own skill and care with respect to its use. Before relying on the material in any important matter, users should carefully evaluate the accuracy, completeness and relevance of the information for their purposes and should obtain appropriate professional advice relevant to their particular circumstances. The material in this book, video file, audio file or any other medium may include views or recommendations of third parties which do not necessarily reflect the views of the author or indicate its commitment to a particular course of action.

External Sites

Any links to other websites are inserted for convenience and do not constitute endorsement of material at those sites or any associated organization, product or service. The listing of a person or company in any part of this website in no way implies any form of endorsement by the author of the products or services provided by that person or company. The author does not have control or responsibility for any external information sources. Links to other websites have been made in good faith in the expectation that the content is appropriately maintained by the author agency/organization and is timely and accurate. It is the responsibility of users/readers to make their own decisions about the accuracy, currency, reliability and correctness of the information at those sites. The author makes no warranties that external information provided from this site is free of infection by computer viruses or other contamination. The author accepts no liability for any interference with or damage to a user's computer, software or data occurring in connection with or relating to this website or its use or any site linked to this site.

Waiver and Release

By accessing information at or through this site each user waives and releases the author to the full extent permitted by law from any and all claims relating to the usage of the material made available through any medium. In no event shall the author be liable for any incident or consequential damages resulting from use of the material.

NOTES

www.CEO-OnDemand.com.au
www.MoreProfitLessTime.com

NOTES

www.CEO-OnDemand.com.au
www.MoreProfitLessTime.com

ACCLAIM FOR **JOHN MILLAR'S**

Business Coaching and Training in their own words....

"Without John Millar as my Business Coach I wouldn't have a business today."

—Grant Jennings Managing Director, Jigsaw Projects

"Taking the decision to be coached and trained by John Millar was carefully considered after experiencing those who over promised and under delivered. I am pleased to say the content of his courses are the tools we all need to master as business owners. His delivery is engaging, thought provoking and empowering and after every session I came away re-energised. John always makes himself available for business building advice both via Skype and face to face beyond the scope of delivery. With his extensive personal experience in building small businesses, he knows and understands what it takes to establish and grow a business.I have no hesitation endorsing John Millar as an educator and business coach and the bonus is he is a very nice person."

—Anne Lederman Managing Director FB Salons

"Johns training with my management team was excellent, it was very different from the business coaching and support I have had in the past. John was clear, thoughtful and he addressed the issues we needed to cover without us even knowing they were being addressed! His follow up has been fantastic and exactly what I needed. I would recommend John and his team to anyone looking at getting some business coaching and training done"

—Wendy Crawford, Peopleworx

"In my dealings with John as our business coach, I have found him to be a motivated and insightful agent of positive change. He is able to burrow down to the root cause of issues and introduce effective forms of measurement. John then identifies and implements practical solutions and is there to provide the gentle persuasion required to ensure that results are achieved."

—Mark Felton, Lindale Insurances

"You have coached and trained us so well throughout the year that we are now used to & find it easy to prepare a 90 day plan, then break it down to actionable bite size pieces. Planning in business & personal life certainly is important. It allows us to identify the important things & the bigger picture. Thank you for your support & guidance throughout the year. And not to mention your insight, external perspective to review & assist our business moving forward."
—**Linda Turner, Director Roy A McDonald Certified Practicing Accountants**

"If you want to achieve sales results you never thought were possible and give your self a competitive edge my strong suggestion is to engage John services and listen closely to what John has to say, during the time I was trained by John I was one of eight sales consultants in a national business for 10 out of the 13 months I lead the sales tally and in 1 quarter I generated three times the revenue of the national sales force combined. Johns training and experience was well worth the investment and paid big dividends. Thanks John."
—**Julian Fadini, Bellvue Capital**

"John is a very enthusiastic trainer and business coach, he is very passionate about getting business owners and their team where they need to be. He goes the extra mile to keep ahead of the latest developments which he then uses to benefit his clients."
—**Darren Reddy CPA**

"I have been to a few seminars and heard John speak numerous times about sales, marketing and business. He is a very knowledgable and extremely enthusiastic business coach in all his interactions and I would recommend him to all business owners who need a sales and marketing boost!"
—**Andrew Heath, Managing Director, Fresh Living Group**

"I worked with John Millar and found his business knowledge, passion and innovation to be inspiring. He has always been able to set (and achieve) strategic long and short-term goals both for himself and his clients without losing that personal connection he builds with everyone he meets. He has been and I believe will continue to be a strong mentor and trainer for anyone wanting to take that next step in their business."
—**Bree Webster, Online Marketing Guru**

"Massive Action Day" – what an understatement, John Millars 4 hour frenzy challenged me to seriously review areas of my business I would not have gone to …. In this way, the process identified incongruence's in my mind, my business and my modus operandi. It's created a paradigm shift. Thanks John, the road map just got a whole lot clearer. Your friendship and insights since 2003 have been a gift to my business and I." —**Andrew Reay, Counsellor, Hypnotherapist and Counsellor, Thinkshift Transformations**

"John Millar is not your usual Business coach or trainer, he gets involved with you and your business and provides hands on help to make sure you follow through on his advice. He is highly motivated to help his clients and his personal guarantee certainly shows this. He has now transposed his thoughts, advice and love of good business onto a series of DVD's in his business venture – More Profit Less Time. This has excellent tips and advice for anyone either starting out or already in business. I highly recommend John to any business owner who wants to run a business and not a j.o.b.!"
—**Darren Cassidy, Managing Director HR2U**

"I and many of my Business Partners and colleagues have worked with John since 2010 as our business oath, trainer and motivator and found him to be an extremely motivational person to assist us achieve our business goals. This company and its products allows for John's skill set to be accessed by a wider number of potential clients. His very professional DVD series is extremely good value for money and is easily accessible for all of us who are time poor. If you are looking to maximise your and your business's results and to start achieving your goals and dreams, contact John; you won't look back!!" —**Mark Cleland, Mortgage Choice**

"John develops real relationships with the people he comes into contact with. He is pasionate about what he does. His DVD and group training series, is full of good ideas and process to make you business better. Knowing what to do and actually doing it are two different things. John is excellent at helping you get things done."
—**Carey Rudd, Sales Director, Online Knowledge**

"I have known John since 2004 and found him to be extremely knowledable in both Sales and Business systems as a business coach without peer. John has provided me with business advice as well as personal coaching over the years, helping me with the running of my organisation. I'm impressed with John's DVD series where he has condensed a lot of the information in an easy to follow format that any business owner can use immediately. I wish he had released these DVDs earlier, as they are a goldmine of information, and practical how to that allow anyone to increase the profit in their business and get back valuable wasted time."

—**Steve Psaradellis, Managing Director, TEBA**

"John's DVD and workbook delivery of his no-nonsense advice provides a low-cost option for those business owners looking to set and achieve goals that will increase profit. I found the conversational style of the DVD's easy to follow, whilst the requirement to pause the DVD and write down some action points ensured a level of commitment to the advice being provided."

—**Mark Felton, Lindale Insurances**

"I only met John briefly at a BNI meeting and knew instantly i need to hire him for my business as my business coach. His attitude towards work and how to improve my cashline had an instant affect on before, even before I finally hired him on an official basis. I found my self thinking "what would John do" and this was only after just meeting him. I can not see my business expend and give me "More Profit Less Time" without John's expert direction and training. If you want to succeed in business life, you need John Millar, without him you're just kidding yourself"

—**Leslie Cachia, Managing Director, Letac Drafting**

"I can highly recommend John Millar to any business owner who wants to grow his business. When I hear very positive feedback from colleagues who are skeptics by nature about John's ability and skills, I know John will help all those he comes in contact with. John comes with a selfless nature and the willingness to work inside a clients business to make it succeed. Rare indeed!"

—**Darren Cassidy, Managing Director, HR2U**

"I first met John Millar in mid 2010 and have always found him to be of an honest and generous character that engenders an easy association with him. I love how easy he is to listen to and how passionate he is about his work and topics. John demonstrates a love for life and his work and I have no hesitation in recommending his services." **—Kathie M Thomas, Managing Director, VA**

"I have listened to John speak on a number of occasions and find him a very knowledgable speaker with a passion for what he does. I have also interacted with a number of his clients and they all tell me that he helps them achieve results in their busienss. If you are looking for business help John is a person you can trust."

—Carey Rudd, Sales Director, Online Knowledge

"John knows his stuff, he knows how the get results, John has so many great ideas in building a business and helping business owners work less and make more money. John has released a DVD set on doing just that. I have watched the 1st one and it was great, very informative and easy to understand, I happily recommend John to anyone in need of help and guidance"

—Frank Eramo, Proprietor, Dynotune

"I have known John only for a short time, however the impact that he has had on me, not just my business has helped me to visualise opportunities that I began to doubt my ability to realise. He is encouraging and at the same time challenging so that he can/you can, begin to see how to maximise the business potential, John calls it being an unreasonable friend, I call it being a mate. If you have any questions about the direction of your business, if you want to seem your bottom line improve not just turnover but real profit, if you want a person who will work with you then I strongly recommend that you engage him at your earliest convenience. John is the best thing that has happened to my business. I could tell you about the way he is on track to make 1/2 a million for me on his contacts alone, but that actually sells him short, he has become like my partner in business, and cares about my success as if it was his own, we will flourish because I took the step to employ his training to help me grow. If you get a chance to get him training you, dont wait like I did, get in as quickly as possible, his time is your business and if like me your business is to make money, then every day you dont have him on retainer you lose money."

—Russell Summers, Managing Director, The Give Life Centre

"Its usually easy to be mediocre in business but it's impossible when you have John Millar training you. He has been my right hand since 2003!" **—David Manser, CFO, Hydrosteer**

"I now have a commercial, profitable business and now its my choice when I work IN my business and when I work ON it and have had john helping me in business since 1988. I cant imagine not having John as a part of our business."
—David Wall, Director, D&K Transport

"The work John has done since 2008 coaching and training our marketing team, administration and finance teams, buyers, store managers and staff nationally has been fantastic."
—Ross Sudano, Director, Anaconda Adventure Stores

"John is a creative, professional, practical and committed business coach and trainer. His approach since we first met him in 1994 to working with a client team through the application of useful tools, information and anecdotes along with his easy going & easy to understand delivery sets him apart from other business coaches that I have used in the past."
—Anthony Beasley, Director, The Astra Group

"I have worked with John Millar for the since 2004 and I didn't think it was possible to achieve what we have achieved together. His business coaching, training and services just get better and better!" **—Terrance Chong, Managing Director, Echo Graphics and Printing**

"John's business coaching, training and support has transformed our business across Australia and New Zealand since 2008."
—Rose Vis, Managing Director, VIP Australia

"We first met John in 2005, he is AMAZING at sales, marketing, operations, logistics, finance training and so much more. Since engaging John as our business coach our business has exploded, our team are happy, our clients are raving about us and my husband and I now take at least 12 weeks holidays a year, EVERY year."
—Shirley Du, Director, Goldline Technology

"It's the no nonsense results driven business coaching and training focus John bought to the table that had such a massive effect on our business."
—David Runkel, Director, Tracomp Fabrication and Steel

"We started working with John in early 2010, within 90 days of working with and being trained by John Millar we had the biggest and most profitable month in our 15 year history. That's impressive."
—Hugh Gilchrist, Managing Director, Australian Moulding Company

If you don't have John as your business trainer you aren't meeting your business potential.
—Don Robertson, Director, Medallion Electrical Services

NOTES

NOTES

NOTES

NOTES

Made in the USA
Columbia, SC
10 October 2024